I KNOW
A BLESSING
WHEN I SEE ONE

CLIFTON JONES

ISBN 978-1-95081-829-7 (paperback)

Copyright © 2019 by Clifton Jones

All rights reserved. No part of this publication may be reproduced, distributed, or transmitted in any form or by any means, including photocopying, recording, or other electronic or mechanical methods without the prior written permission of the publisher. For permission requests, solicit the publisher via the address below.

Rushmore Press LLC
1 888 733 9607
www.rushmorepress.com

Printed in the United States of America

PROLOGUE

The weather forecaster was on a hot streak. Once again, the evening had turned out to be an unseasonably comfortable. In mid-June when the temperatures were normally a hot muggy 95 degrees today only peaked at a surprisingly 78 degrees with a nice gentle breeze coming out of the south.

As I stepped out on the grounds of one of my best friend's homes, it still amazed me how well he was doing and living for that matter. I had just pulled up into his driveway and gotten out of my car expecting his huge dog to come bouncing across the yard at me. I remember the first time I saw the mixed breed giant playing in the yard with my friend. Rolling and tugging at each other as if they had no other cares in the world. This was quite a sight because Buford was part bloodhound and a bull mastiff. I used to worry a bit about my friend's safety after he told me how he got Buford from an animal shelter where had been brought in after being found in terrible shape. He was changed to a post by a former owner. They had even considered putting him down because of his aggressive nature whenever someone tried to put a leash on him, but my friend insisted that all Buford needed was love.

The sound of his barking quickly brings me back to the present moment, and I catch sight of the huge dog galloping toward me. Believe me when I say that it's enough to alarm anyone. I almost turned to get back inside the safe confines of my car and honk the horn until my friend comes out, but before I can, Buford slightly slows and then suddenly changes direction and head back to the direction he came. As I began to hurriedly walk towards the door,

Buford returns with, of all things, my friend's grandson riding on his bike. I knew then that everything was okay.

The child waved at me and as I waved back, my good friend walks from around the house smiling broadly at me, waving me over. We cordially greet each other with our customary handshake and half hug. He offers me a seat on his screened porch. We sit in his custom-made Morris chairs and watch Buford and Excel play in the front yard.

"So, how's it going Steve?" my friend asks.

"It's well as can be expected. I was passing through town when I saw that the parking lot in front of the laundromat was full so I decided to stop by and visit one of the newest success stories in our area."

With a slight shaking of his head and an offset grin he replies, "See what the Lord has done."

"Yeah, but you helped, right?", I said.

"Wrong", he said. "I wasn't able to even help myself survive all that I went through. It was He alone who did it all for me. He gets all the accolades not me."

"You always say that, but you've got to see that your willingness played apart", I replied.

"You still don't get it do you, Steve?" He rises from his seat and opens his front door to the entrance of his home and yells to his daughter, "KJ, would you bring a pitcher of ice tea and lemons to the porch for me and Mr. Steve? Thank you, Honey."

I give him that look as he sits back down. "What!" he says. "Why do you insist on calling me, Mister?' I ask.

"It's not me", he begins, "It's the way she's been raised. That's you that doesn't like the sound of it because it makes you feel old".

"And I'm not old", I quickly interject.

"Humph, let you tell it. What are you anyway? Forty pushing sixty".

"Hey" is all I can say, but my friend doesn't let up.

"Wasn't that a bottle of Just for Men I saw in your car the other day? Let's face it, Steve, your gray hair is like bad grass, the more you cut it the more of it grows back. But in your case, its grays".

"Well, at least I have hair baldly," I replied.

"I have hair", he says, "You just can't see it!"

We both laughed as KJ comes out with a tray of ice tea and a bowl of mixed nuts. She greets me with a hug and asks me how have I been doing? His father quickly responds, "He's doing great for an old fart like him."

"Poppa stop", she tells him.

"Excel, get ready to come inside for your bath, okay!"

"In a little while momma. Buford and I are playing." Little Excel tells his mother and Buford actually seems to bark in agreement.

"Baby girl, I'll send him into you in a minute." her father says.

"Okay, poppa. Oh, by the way, momma said you need to make sure you call her tonight at 8:30 pm sharp and don't be late". She bends over and kisses her father on top of his head, and as she turns back to go into the house, my friend smartly replies, "I'm always on time, it's your momma who's too early."

We all laugh and KJ returns to her cooking. I look at my friend in awe and I realize just how fortunate he really is. Or as he would say, "I'm blessed." I still find myself wondering how he made it through all the horrors he's faced but that only figures into the end of the story. This is how it all started.

CHAPTER 1

"Damn! How did I get myself into this mess?" Shelia dabbed at her now tear dampened face. She frowned at the tracks where her mascara had run after her fit of crying.

"Get a hold of yourself girl", she replied as she stared at her reflection in the mirror. "You can get through this", she told herself. "It's only a pregnancy, right? People get pregnant every day, right? Hell, it happens to everybody."

As she tried to rationalize her plight all over again for the umpteenth time during the past eight and a half months. The question of how she could have let this happen echoes in her mind. She gently strokes her very swollen belly knowing that in just a few more days a drastic change would occur in her life. A baby. A baby in her life. Not someone else's baby, but her very own baby in her already unstable life. As she sat on the edge of the bathtub as if on cue, her baby moved or kicked or whatever as if to remind her just how real her situation was.

"You're messing up my plan ya know that!" as she spoke to her stomach in a rather loud voice. Shelia's frustration with herself was becoming more real and more apparent as her due date got closer.

Her friends were for the most part supportive knowing that many other young girls had had babies before marriage. Some even managed quite well for themselves, but this was different. Sheila was different. A baby did not fit into her plans. Her future was not geared to revolve around becoming a mother. She was smart and she knew it. Her grade point average along with her acceptance into the Xavier

University of New Orleans was proof that she was made of the kind of stuff it took to make it in this world.

Times were changing. Colored folk was starting to get the opportunities they'd always dreamed of but up until recently been denied. She'd watched the march on Washington, witnessed the boycotts, even took part in a couple of "C.O.R.E" sits ins. Yeah, times were changing and doors were opening. She couldn't, wouldn't blow her chance at success by being shackled down by an unwanted pregnancy. Not now, with everything about to change for the better. She'd seen enough of the sharecropper's lifestyle which was no life at all. No, she was buying into her mother's and aunt's dreams of her marrying and settling down to raise God to know how many kids in an old raggedy-ass shotgun house. Her thoughts raced inside her head as she finished dressing trying to remember all of the places she had to go before she reported to her afternoon class. She passed through the living room of the one-bedroom apartment that she shared with her older cousin who worked at the brewery. She worked there on a part-time basis but now was on leave because of her baby. There were bills due in a couple of weeks and without her check to help, her cousin would really be pressed to make the weight. She closed and locked the door behind her and proceeded to walk her normal route to the bus stop.

"Damn it's hot this morning," she heard one colored man tell his friend as she passed them by.

"Sheila, you ain't had that baby yet?!!"

That was Raymond Brown who lived a couple of houses down from where she and her cousin lived. The whole street was lined with duplex houses and Raymond was the local "Mr. Fix It" for every woman in the neighborhood. He was a good guy even though he was an all-out skirt chaser. He'd tried to get close to her before she started blowing up like she'd swallowed a watermelon seed. But at least she hadn't had to worry about any of his unwanted advances for the last six months. That was a relief by itself.

"Believe me, I can't wait to get this thing outta me," Sheila said. "It's slowing me down entirely too much! My jiggle done turned into a wobble!"

I KNOW A BLESSING WHEN I SEE ONE

Both men let out a howl at the joke that Sheila made and watch as she walks away quickly as the bus rounds the corner and begins to slow as it approaches its stop. Several patrons are for the bus and a couple that slowed the process of getting on the bus giving Sheila a chance to make it. Once she'd dropped her tokens in the slot, she began to look for a place to sit because her feet had remained swollen from the night before and she needed to rest. The bus was unusually crowded this morning and none of the men looked to be in the gentlemen mood to give up their seat for her. Just as she had resigned to the idea of having to stand up, she noticed that a lady was waving at her trying to get her attention to come sits in the empty seat next to her. Sheila hesitated, even though her feet were aching and that seat looked so inviting, yet she didn't want to sit by the lady whose smile was so warm and tender. She was a nun.

"Oh, what the hell," Sheila sighed and as the nun moved over, she eased down next to her and readied herself for the oncoming conversation. Sheila was never much at a religious person in the way everybody thought she ought to be. She believed God was there and that He created everything. She also believed that God let people make their own way easy or hard. She believed that anyone's life could be made better if they worked hard.

She didn't hold well with the idea of the white folks thinking that they were better than she was. She'd worked hard and learned a lot. That fact alone brought forth the results of being in college now. Hell, there were several white kids whose parents Sheila's mother had worked for that she tutored in several subjects helping them get through junior high. As she sat there remembering these days in Mrs. Wilson's den, working with those kids. She would make up different learning games to help them remember certain math formulas. They would laugh and talk together, and they would be so excited to show her their test scores. The improvements made her proud as a mother hen. Such wonderful moments where everyone in there were all equal were completely overshadowed by the sobering truth that they weren't allowed to even acknowledge her or what she'd been to them in any public setting. This was one of the many reasons she had to finish school, get out of the south and try to make some of her dreams come true. But right now, all of that was threatened by this baby.

"Hi, my name is Sister Katie," the nun said as she offered her hand to Sheila. Sheila timidly responded and shook the nun's hand. "So, I see that you're pretty well along. How soon will it be?" Sister Katie had a cute round face that looked sincere to Sheila so she allowed herself to be drawn into the conversation.

"I'm in my ninth month. I'm due in a couple of weeks."

"Oh my," sister Katie exclaimed. "You shouldn't even be walking from place to place in your condition." The more this nun spoke, Sheila realized that she wasn't from these parts, mainly due to her accent or lack of one, and her reaction to her condition as she put it.

"That's why I'm on the bus sitting by you." She realized she'd been a bit sarcastic in her response, but the nun just kept on talking as if she didn't notice, or wasn't offended. Sheila looked at the woman and found herself wondering what color she was. She looked white and had light brown eyes with a few scattered freckles spread across her cheekbones. She very well could be white, but here in New Orleans, she'd met colored people who could "pass" with ease. They were the high mixed ones of usually French and Indian descent with what seemed to be just a few drops of colored blood in them. But in the south, these couple of drops were more than enough to be classified as colored. Sheila tore herself from those thoughts and refocused her attention on this num that she couldn't tell what color she was and why was she so talkative. As if reading her mind, sister Katie blushed and said, "Forgive me, I tend to over talk myself", as the other sisters say. "But it does help when I'm working at the hospital."

This point interested Sheila and she ventured to ask what did she do at the hospital. "I split my duties between post-surgical aftercare and prenatal care," Katie responded.

"That must take a lot of you having to work at the hospital and serve at the church," Sheila said.

"Well, it's a bit rough at times, but it's rewarding, to say the least," was Katie's response. Sheila detected a hint of something in Katie's voice that made her even more curious. As the bus made yet another stop, she plunged in with a question.

"You seem a bit, discouraged sister. You do like what you're doing, don't you?" Sheila asked.

"Oh yes, yes." Katie adamantly stated. "I just wish that I could do more for the patients and what they need."

"What do you mean to do more, there's only so much you can do right? I mean you can only do so much in your position, right?"

"It's hard for me? Sometimes I can't imagine how you and all of your people made it down here." Katie replied.

"Well sister", Sheila said, "this ain't heaven on earth for us colored folks. I can tell you that much."

Katie turned and faced Sheila and said "Y'know back where I come from it's not like this. Times have changed and black people have so many opportunities."

"Black people, is that what they call us where you're from?" Sheila asked.

"Yes, they do. Back in California people don't act so cruel and heartless as I've seen down here." Katie looked out of the window and softly murmured, "It's enough to make anybody ask where God is in the middle of all this." Sheila placed her hand on Katie's should as if to say I'm glad somebody understands.

They looked at each other and smiled. Right then at that very moment, each knew that a friendship had been born.

"So, what are you hoping for?" Katie asked Sheila.

"Oh, let's see" as Sheila began to count off on her fingers, "one, a quick delivery, two a quick delivery with as fewer amounts of pain as possible, and to get my shape back to normal size."

"No silly", Katie exclaimed. "I mean the baby. Do you want a boy or a girl?" This was it. She'd rehearsed in her mind a thousand times that she didn't want this baby, that she would give it up. These were all thoughts that had never been voiced before until now. Sheila tried to swallow the lump that was forming in her throat. She cleared her throat and mumbled that sounded to Katie like I don't want it.

"I'm sorry Sheila, I couldn't understand you. What did you just say?" Katie asked.

"I, I don't really……it doesn't matter to me. I'm not keeping it. I'm not ready for children yet. Maybe not ever." Sheila replied.

Katie stared dumbfounded at her new friend not realizing that this newly birthed friendship was already facing its first major test for survival. How in the world could a healthy, vibrant young woman not want her own baby? She thought. She looked at Sheila's hand and for the first time noticed she didn't have a wedding ring on her finger or even the print of one for that matter that would normally be left on the finger of the owner. She now looked at the cold shock of now knowing that Sheila was unwed and faced becoming an unwed mother in less than two short weeks. Sheila sat silently watching this nun struggle with her emotions. The bus began to slow and stopped at the Tulane bus stop.

"Well, it was nice meeting your sister, and thanks for the seat," Sheila said.

"Wait, this is my stop, too. Are you going inside?" Katie asked.

"Yeah, I have a doctor's appointment." Sheila turned to walk away when Katie quickly caught up to her, slipped something in her pocket as she hugged and said "I'll see you soon."

CHAPTER 2

"Well young lady, everything including you and the baby seems to be in good condition." The doctor had just read the results of the blood work tests and was signing off on the bottom of Sheila's chart when he turned towards her and said, "In just a couple more weeks you will be ripe for the picking."

Sheila ignored the degrading remark and continued to button up her blouse. She was on her last button when she stepped from behind the petition. What was on her mind was what she would do after the baby was born.

"Well, I guess you're ready to be on your way," the doctor said as she got up from the small white desk in the corner of the examination room.

"Yeah, I guess so," she replied as he opened the door to let her out. "Uh, Doc, I gotta question for you". Sheila said hesitantly.

"Well, make it snappy. I've got a whole mess of you gals waiting to be seen. Y'all got to learn to keep ya dresses down. You coloreds are making babies fastern' you can care for 'em."

Sheila's ears were burning which was always a sure sign that she was in a rage. She glared at the doctor as if bullets would explode from her eyes and rip through his chest and penetrate his heart bringing to end what she believed to be a shallow existence. He coughed and you could hear the strain that was on his lungs, results from smoking cigarettes over 35 years at least. She looked at him with disgust as she said in her head for at least the third time today, "And you call yourself a doctor."

He repositioned his glasses while he rested his eyes on her milk swollen breasts, but quickly turned away as Sheila caught him again. Man, this guy was a real jackass, but the clinic was so understaffed and even fewer doctors wanted it to be known that they touched pregnant colored girls for that matter. Their public appearance had to be kept even though behind closed doors. Well, that was a horse of a different color.

"Well, spit it out. What's your question?"

"I was wondering", Sheila began, "If there was anything, I could do to get rid of this baby. You know after I have it and all?"

"What do you mean get rid of it? Isn't this your first child? Why on earth would you want to up and do that for?" the doctor asked.

"The reason why doesn't matter. The question is how can I get rid of it!??" Sheila could feel her anger rising and she'd already had a couple of minor instances where her blood pressure shot up due to prenatal stress. "But the nerve of the guy", Sheila thought, "trying to get all up in my business."

"I guess the next things you'll want to know is who the daddy is?" said Sheila.

At that moment, one of the nurses walked up to the propped open-door hearing Sheila's raised voice. She looked pointedly at Sheila and asked, "Is there a problem Dr. Gray?"

"Humph!" was the only sound that Sheila made as she leaned onto the examining table with her arms crossed with no intention of being moved.

"No problem Maggie. Just this young lady has a few questions I need to answer for her." He said.

"Well, are you sure because I could stay," the nurse replied.

"No need for you to stay in here with me Maggie. I need you to have the next patient put in room #3 and I'll be there shortly okay?" The nurse gave Sheila a long look that Sheila returned with a bit of eye-rolling.

"If you need me doctor, just buzz," the nurse told Dr. Gray as she backed out of the room.

"Don't worry honey, I'll keep the good doctor safe," Sheila said with a wink at the departing nurse that caused her to turn red. She shut the door a bit too forcefully causing a couple of wall pictures to shake.

"I'm sorry Dr. Gray. I'm just under a lot of pressure right now with me trying to go to school and all, it's just a bit hard!" Sheila almost sobbed out her last words. She was amazed at how quickly her emotions had changed.

"Damn, this baby has got me all out of control," she thought as she took a handkerchief from her purse to wipe away her tears.

"Oh no, now. Don't you go and start all that crying? You'll have this whole place overrunning with a flood if the rest of them gals see you and get started. Besides, then I'll have to call Maggie because I can't swim!" Sheila laughed at Dr. Gray's little joke. "Now that better." Said the doctor.

"So how long have you known that you didn't want to keep your baby?" His question seemed straight forward enough so Sheila decided to put aside her pride and tell Dr. Gray her situation.

"Dr. Gray", Sheila began, "I'm the first person in my entire family who has finished high school. I'm a freshman at Xavier and I have some major plans for my life. I want to graduate and become a journalist and leave the south and travel all over, writing the kind of stories people want to read about. I didn't plan this. Hell, I didn't want this. I didn't use protection and now I'm paying for it. But I'm not gonna pay the same price forever!" Sheila paused as her bottom lip began to tremble which was a sure sign that a crying spell was close behind.

"When you say you're not going to pay the price forever, exactly what do you mean by that?" Dr. Gray asked. He had suddenly become quite interested in the plight of this young high-strung colored girl who just happened to be pregnant.

"I mean that I can lose all of my hopes and dreams if I even try to entertain the idea of raising a child." Sheila was exasperated. "How could I make this man understand my situation," she thought. "Maybe after I completed school and working at a newspaper, then I could get married and have a child, but not now." She found herself standing up and grabbing her purse again.

"Y'know young lady, there are a lot of people who would love to be in your shoes. There are a lot of young families starting that would jump at the chance to have a baby." Dr. Gray replied.

"Well, where are they because as God is my judge," Sheila said as she raised her right hand, "they can have this one."

As she opened the door to leave Dr. Gray said, "That baby could be a blessing from the Lord."

"I know a blessing when I see one, and this ain't it!"

CHAPTER 3

"Sheila girl, come on in here and help me get these clothes ready to wash."

"Shit!" Sheila cursed under her breath. "I'm coming Wanda, gimme a minute I got to go pee. Damn, I'll be glad when all this shit is over", Sheila pushed her way up from the couch and hurried to the bathroom. She had to pass through her cousin Wanda's room on her way there. "One-minute girl", she motioned and Wanda, as she, in turn, threw a rolled-up pair of socks at Sheila.

"Girl, you been running to that bathroom a lot, you sho yo water ain't done broke?"

"Hell no", Sheila yelled back from the bathroom. "Even though it feels like a damn waterfall coming out of me." Wanda laughed at Sheila's comment, shaking her head at the same time. She heard the toilet flush as Sheila came wobbling out. "Wanda, tell the truth. Was it this bad when you had Calvin?" Sheila plopped down on the side of the bed next to Wanda and started separating the colored clothes from the whites. As she did this, she thought, "Even the colored clothes can't mix with the whites."

"It was worse with Calvin," Wanda retorted. "And Lord have mercy when I had him. Do you see how big that head is uh, he is? That child damn near kilt me!" Both women burst into laughter.

"Girl, you ought not to talk about Calvin like that." Sheila teased.

"I had em and as long as he mine, I can say what I want!"

"Girl, the Lord gone punish you fo' talkin' bout that boy that way. You oughta be shame a yo'self". Said Sheila.

"I ain't ashamed," Wanda replied as she tossed a dirtied work jumpsuit in the basket after checking the pockets. "I wasn't ashamed when I laid there and made him and I ain't shame that he's mine."

"Even tho' Uncle Joe and Aunt Sis act as he does," Sheila threw in. "Chile, I remember when you told Aunt Sis you were pregnant with Calvin. Why I thought she was gone have a heart attack right then, and Lord doesn't talk about Uncle Joe." Uncle Joe said, "If you ain't planning on getting married, then you gonna have to find you somewhere else to stay, cause I ain't takin' care of you and some negroes baby."

"Well, least he wasn't lyin'," Wanda said. "After he put me out and I went to live with Ms. Mamie an 'em, momma would come over there every day to see about me." Daddy stayed mad with me up until Calvin was born."

"Didn't he come to the hospital fussin'?" asked Sheila

"Yea girl. Makin all that noise and as soon as he saw Calvin, he whatn't madder after that!" Wanda grinned as the memories came back to her.

"They gonna let Calvin come stay with you next week, right?" Sheila asked while she went through the pockets of her jean jacket.

"They betta! Act like that's the child." Wanda replied.

"What's this?" Wanda reached down to the floor to pick up a piece of paper that fell out of Sheila's jacket.

"What's what?" Sheila said as she took the paper that Wanda reached to her. As she unfolded it, there inside was the name of a church with sister Katie's name on it. How did she get this?" She must have slipped this in my pocket while she hugged me." There was a phone number with a message that read, "Your Blessing Is On The Way."

"What'd it says, Sheila?" Wanda asked.

It says, "Your Blessing Is On The Way." Sheila smiled in a sarcastic way as she placed her hand on her stomach for emphasis. Wanda just slowly shook her head.

"Whose name is on the paper?" Wanda pressed on.

"My, we sho is mighty curious this evening ain't we?" Sheila sat back before Wanda could take the paper out of her hand.

"Because you are my favorite cousin and I promised yo momma 'em that I wouldn't let nothing happen to you while you were living with me. That includes you running away to God knows where with that baby in yo arms." Wanda folded her arms under her large breasts looking a whole lot like Sheila's momma.

"Mo like me running without if you ask me," Sheila said.

"Well, it sounds to me that you still don't know what you want to do about this baby, but I know one thing you better make up your mind soon because it will be here, real son. Now back to the name." She got up and quickly snatched the folded paper out of Sheila's hand and read the name aloud, "Sister Katie. Who's she?" Wanda asked.

"Just someone I met the other day on the bus on my way to the clinic. She's a num who works at the hospital and we talked, we laughed, she hugged me by and some kinda way slipped this note into my pocket. End of story. Satisfied, dear Abbey?"

"Not quite." Was Wanda's response. "What does she do at the hospital? She asked while tying the white dirty closes up in the sheet.

"She works in the delivery room or baby's ward or something like that! Here, let me help you." Sheila reached to pick up the other bundles of clothes left on the floor.

"I got this stuff," Wanda said. "What I need you to do is take this paper and call this sister Katie and invite her over for dinner tomorrow night."

"For what? You don't even know her." Sheila exclaimed.

"That's why I want you to invite her over because I want to get to know her. I got some religious questions that she might answer."

"What kinda questions and since when you so interested in the church?" Sheila asked. "As a matter of fact, whatn't you who Aunt Sis had to drag to church and then once you got there the minute, she turned her back, you were out of the back door hanging out with that fat ass Amy Sims? I bet you don't remember one sermon the preacher gave either".

Wanda put the bundle of clothes in the shopping cart that she had conveniently borrowed from the parking lot of A&P. "First of all, I do remember a couple of sermons Rev. Jones preached on. Secondly, I wasn't always hanging with Amy Simms. That girl would have ruined my good saintly reputation." Sheila hocked at that. Wanda paid no attention to her cousin and went right along with her explanation. "Third, it doesn't matter what I did back then anyway. It only matters what I do now that makes a difference".

"You still ain't answered my question." Sheila insisted.

"You just invite her over and you'll find out." With that, Wanda pushed the cart out the door.

CHAPTER 4

"Sister Katie, you must remember what our true purpose here in this hospital."

"Oh yes, Reverend Mother. Our goal is to meet and supply the needs of those who are unfortunate just as our Lord Jesus would have." Katie responded a bit too fast as she realized her mistake as the Reverend Mother slowed her pace in the halls of the hospital to glance at her whom she considered the very young, inexperienced and naïve sister Katie. Once a week, the hospital nurses were visited by the Reverend Mother to find out if the needed anything to aid them in their ministry to the less fortunate. Unfortunately, these visits were actually the Reverend Mother's way of scrutinizing all the new or young nuns in the parish. This was quite stressful to sister Katie and if the truth were to be known to the majority of the nuns who served at the hospital. It wasn't that they did things wrong, but they could never do enough things right, that is in the eyes of the Reverend Mother. Today was no different.

"Sister Katie you seem a bit anxious today. Is there a reason for this show of haste?" asked the Reverend Mother.

"No Reverend Mother. It's just that I was thinking about what we do here and what differences we make in the lives of the patients. There are so many people who are suffering due to lack and right now we're seeing an influx of unwed mothers." Sister Katie explained.

The Reverend Mother stopped completely this time and faced, sister Katie. This always made every hospital attendant nervous as if they were all back in grade school standing before the vice principal's desk waiting for some form of condemnation to fall due to whatever was done wrong.

"I suppose you would have a more socialistic or as you've put it in the past modern approach to this problem." Reverend Mother said.

"Actually, I would think that we need to approach this dilemma with more of a bird's eye view or so to speak. With the numbers increasing as he is, I fear that if some new form of solution is not factored in then we're going to be faced with a whole new generation of children being raised b single parents." Sister Katie concluded in what felt like one complete breath.

"So, what would you suggest? I hope to God you're not building up the nerve to purpose any form of contraceptive other than abstinence." The Reverend Mother warned.

"Oh, land sakes, God forbid Reverend Mother. That's the furthest thing from my mind." Sister Katie retorted. "My suggestion is that we would begin to help these girls who are now in these predicaments make the right decisions for the best interest of the child."

"Please, sister Katie. I have a lot of things to do this morning so why don't you say what's on your mind!" said Reverend Mother.

"I've come across several families you wouldn't mind becoming adoptive parents to some of these children. I may even know of a few girls that could be helped." At that moment, her mind flashed back to her meeting with Sheila for that first time. Ever since that morning, she'd hoe to have Sheila contact her. "OH, why didn't I just give the note to her outright, instead of slipping it in her pocket. She probably washed it already in her laundry." She thought.

"Sister Katie, are you aware of how much research it takes to make sure that a couple is fit to be adoptive parents? This is not an easy task you would suggest. Yet, I do see the wisdom in it. I tell you what since you've already begun the necessary research for such a project, I give you the approval, to begin with, one of the young women who do not wish to be a mother at this time in their lives." The Reverend Mother concluded and turned continuing on her rounds.

I KNOW A BLESSING WHEN I SEE ONE

"Yes, Reverend Mother, I'll get right on it and I promise you won't be disappointed." Sister Katie chirped along as she stepped quickly to keep up.

"That I can believe." Said Reverend Mother.

CHAPTER 5

Sheila sat in the waiting room with her legs crossed while sweat ran down the back of her calves. She'd just finished filling out the proper forms to apply for the financial aid she'd have to have if she wound u keeping this baby. Her day had been a pretty rough one and right now she wished more than ever to be a back at home with her feet soaking in a pan of hot water and Epson salt.

"Number 26!" the lady behind the counter yelled. Sheila hopped up and made her way to the counter. She handed the lady her ticket and then her forms.

"Everything seems to be in order. Is there someone we can contact if you're accepted?"

"Yes, my cousin Wanda, that's who I live with," Sheila said.

"Yes, I see. Ok, now what about the father of your child? Will he be trying to live with you?" the worker asked.

"No, ma'am. He and I are not together. So, I'm completely by myself." Sheila stated.

"What about me, Sheila. I count as somebody, right?" Sheila whirled around to see, sister Katie.

"Hey, Katie! What are you doing here?" Sheila gave Katie a hug and the two were about to walk off when Sheila remembered the social worker. "Give me a minute Katie to take care of this little matter". She told Katie. "Now back to you. Is there anything else that I need to fill out?" Sheila asked the social worker.

"Everything's complete. I do have you scheduled to talk to Mr. Tanner regarding our inquiries for foster care." Said the social worker. She reached Sheila a slip of paper with the office address and telephone number to get in contact with Mr. Tanner.

"Thank you for your time," Sheila said over her shoulder as she went to meet Katie at the door. "So, what are you doing here?" She asked again.

"I had to drop off some medical records to the department head that I'd been researching for a new project I've been given," Katie told Sheila as they walked down the hall of the hospital.

"As a matter of fact, I was hoping to see you again, and here you are," Katie said.

"Yeah, well I was about to call you even though I can't imagine for the life of me how I got or phone number in my coat pocket." Sheila threw in.

"Oh, that. Well, I'm sorry about that but I didn't quite know how to get in contact with you and I just meeting you didn't want to make you feel pressured with my overbearing self."

"Well if I didn't know any better, Sister Katie, I'd think that you had some experience in being a pickpocket" Shelia teased.

Katie turned red and exclaimed, "Oh heavens no. I didn't mean to come across like that. I just…. I really wanted to get to know you better."

"Katie, I'm just pickin' at you. I'm glad to see you too. As a matter of fact, I am formally inviting you to my house for dinner with me and my cousin Wanda." Sheila said.

"That would be wonderful! When, where and what time?" Katie asked.

"How about tomorrow night at about seven? Here's our address. Look, I gotta go, so I'll see you then, okay?" She said rushing off.

"I'll see you tomorrow Sheila, God Bless!" Katie yelled after her new friend. She looked towards the sky and said to herself, "I see your blessing is on the way, Lord. Thank you." She hurriedly returned to her duties in the newborn ward on the second floor. Katie realized that what she was thinking could be wrong, but deep down in her heart she knew that she was right about Sheila. She knew that this young, vibrant woman needed another chance to start over. The thing that would be hard is to convince her that the best decision would be for her to keep the child. But if she was settled in her heart not to keep the child, then certainly it would be better to give the child up for adoption rather than foster care. Yes, the more the thought about the matter, she was confident that all this was God's doing for her to be a blessing to Sheila in her time of need and to give that baby the chance to be the blessing to someone else's future. With that thought, the rest of her day flew by.

"Sheila, you in here?" Wanda called out as she entered the house with an armload of groceries.

"In here, cuz," Sheila yelled back. Wanda kicked the door closed, dropped the two sacks of groceries not too gently on the sofa and then she plopped down in the adjoining armchair.

"Whew, what a day. Child, I thought I'd never get home on time tonight. The mid-day shift was short three workers and I had to stay an extra hour to help thins along. Then the bus was late and I barely made it to A&P's on time. It's just been one damn thing after another!" Wanda relayed all this information while pulling her work shorts off, then her socks. She stretched out as far as could in the armchair until it creaked under the stress.

"Sorry, your day was so bad cuz. Let me put these groceries up." Sheila said as she awkwardly lifted the bags from the sofa.

"Thanks, sweetie," Wanda said. "My day wasn't too bad. It just got really hectic from in the end. Looked like all hell was gonna break lose at any minute."

Well, I'm just glad the hell didn't break out with you around. Can't have nothing happening to my favorite cousin, now can we?" Sheila yelled from the kitchen. She put the bread in the bread box on the counter cabinet then took out the rest of the food items and placed them in their proper places. When she finished, she went back to dicing onions and bell peppers for the gravy she was making. She lowered the fire under the black cast-iron skillet, grabbed a towel and took the skillet in one hand and with the other held the top in place as she drained the grease off the fried pork chops that she had been preparing. She glanced at eh clock on the wall. It was six o'clock and Katie would be here around seven. She'd called earlier to confirm that she was still coming as planned and that she was excited to meet

Wanda and she said she wanted to share something important with me. This last part made her a bit nervous. She put her skillet back on the burner then she added a cup of water along with the onions and bell pepper. The aroma began almost instantly as the skillet began to simmer. Now she could get back to making sure the rest of the meal would be right. Along with the pork chops they were having steamed rice, French green beans, and cornbread and there was apple flavored bread pudding cooling on the opposite counter next to the refrigerator.

"Girl, what you cooking got the house smelling all good?" Wanda yelled from the room.

"Shit!" Sheila swore. She'd forgotten to tell Wanda that she'd talked to Katie yesterday and that she had invited her to have dinner with them tonight. By the time she got up this morning, Wanda was already gone to work. "Wanda", Sheila called as she gingerly walked into her cousin's bedroom. "I forgot to tell you that we got company coming tonight. I did like you asked and invited sister Katie for dinner." She waited for Wanda's outburst.

"What time she supposed to be here?" Wanda called back through the bathroom door. She'd already started her bath and hopefully, Sheila thought, she'd be relaxed enough not to be overly testy around Katie.

"She said to look for her around seven or a little after. I meant to tell you but it kinda slipped my mind with all the things that have been going on lately."

Wanda burst out the door with a plastic bag tied around her head to protect her hair from getting wet and water dripping from her naked body as she hurriedly patted herself dry. She sat in a chair and dried her feet and ushered Sheila out of the room with a wave of her hand while saying, "Get your tail, back in that kitchen befo' you be done burnt up the food. It'd be a terrible thing for her to come and eat yo' burnt cookin'! Now go, I'll be out in a minute." Wanda announced.

"Yes, ma'am!" Sheila said with a smile and flew back to the kitchen.

The table was set and everything looked lovely. Sheila was so thankful that instead of being angry with her for not telling her that Katie was coming tonight, Wanda joined in after she'd gotten dressed and helped tidy up the living room and the bathroom. Sheila recalled the words that her momma drilled in her regarding keeping a clean house. "People can always tell if you are a clean person by the way you keep your bathroom. They'll smile in your face and the minute they get out of hearing distance; they'll talk about you like a dog!" her momma would say. Sheila looked over at Wanda as she re-fluffed the pillows on the sofa. She even noticed that she was even humming along with the Supremes on the radio.

"Child, that's Diana Ross know she can sing. She not too cut but she can sing!" Wanda said as she started to rearrange the plastic centerpiece on the table for the third time.

"Wanda, what gives you gives? Why you so happy? Acting like you on cloud 9 or something." Sheila asked.

"Nothing, just anxious to meet the good sister," Wanda replied.

At that very moment, the baby kicked and it almost startled Sheila. It had been very quiet for the last couple of days, but for the last couple of hours, you'd think it was trying to make his grand appearance now instead of arriving when he was expected. "Dang", Sheila said speaking to her stomach. "You act like you wanna be the guest of honor at the little dinner party."

"Sheila, you said something?" Wanda called out from the living room. She'd tired of checking everything and had settled in front of the little black and white Curtis Mathis to watch tonight's episode of Gunsmoke.

"Just talking to myself" answered Sheila.

"Long as you don't start answering yo'self back, then I'm getting outta here!" said Wanda.

"Don't worry. That ain't about to happen." Sheila walked over to sit down and watch television with Wanda when there was a soft knock at the door. Both women jumped and hurried towards the door.

"Let me get it, Wanda!" Sheila said pushing past her cousin.

"It's my house ain't it?" Wanda responded.

"Yo house, my friend. Now what?!" Sheila retorted.

Wanda turned to go back to her place on the couch and muttered just loud enough for Sheila to hear. "Go head witcha' black tail. Humph. Makes me sick!"

Sheila looked back over her shoulder and stuck her tongue out at Wanda just as she began to open the door. Katie stood on the threshold of the duplex with a smile bright as a hundred-watt light bulb. Sheila noticed at that moment how everything was. "Even the white folks around here didn't keep their teeth up that well. She's got to be from California or someplace like that." Sheila mused to herself.

"Good evening sister Katie. Welcome to our humble abode." Sheila announced with a wave of her hand ushering Katie inside.

Katie walked inside, turned back to face Sheila and said, "Now that I'm here you can cut the crap!"

Wanda hooped with laughter and got up to meet this woman who left her cousin sanding there totally speechless. Katie turned to face Wanda extending her hand, palm upward, and said "You must be Wanda, give me some skin sista?"

Now it was Wanda's turn to be stunned, but hers lasted only a moment and she slapped Katie on her palm and said, "Right on sista!" Then the two women began to talk as if they were long lost friends amid a reunion. They both went and sat down on the couch while Sheila continued to stare at the both of them in amazement. It was Wanda who came up for air first and said, "Sheila, what's wrong with you? Actin' all is strange. Pay her no mind, Katie, she gets like that sometimes. Her mind just drifts off like a sailboat on the ocean, poor thang'!" Wanda began to tease, but Sheila fired right back ready for the challenge.

"What I wanna know is why you tryin' to sho' me up in front of the company, Ms. Thank?!"

"Aint nobody showin' you up, you just made me and my new soul sista is connectin'!" Wanda responded.

"Hey, there's enough time for everybody to get to know each other. What I wanna know is what y'all get to eat around here?" Katie exclaimed. "I ain't had no real food since I left home!"

"Well honey, don't say another word, come on Sheila let's put some food on the table and feed our starvin' sista befo' she faints!" Wanda shouted as she got up and she and Sheila headed towards the kitchen.

"Y'all let me help. It feels like it's been a million years since I been able to relax and just be me." Katie reached up to her head and took off her head covering placing it on the coffee table and then hurriedly followed into the kitchen behind Sheila and Wanda.

"Ooh girl, it smells good up in here. Is that stewed pork chops I smell? Lord have mercy child. I know I gon' eat good tonight!" Katie exclaimed.

Sheila was helping Wanda bring the food to the table and was on her way back from the dining room table when she noticed that Katie had removed the customary headwear that nuns wore. She also noticed that Katie had a head full of coal-black hair that was so curly that it could be called kinky.

"Girl you ain't gon' get in trouble for takin' that thing off in here?" Wanda questioned. She too had stopped from pouring the pork chops into a serving dish and staring at this very interesting house guest that was becoming more surprising by the moment.

"Now, it's not as I had on a customary habit or anything like that," Katie said in a rather flat tone. She walked over to the stove where the skillet of cornbread was kept warm, reached over to her left into the cabinet, took a plate and placed it on top of the cornbread, grabbed a towel and expertly gripped the skillet handle with her right hand and holding the plate in place with her left. She then flipped the cornbread onto the plate, set the now-empty skillet back down and proceeded to take the cornbread to the table. Wanda and Sheila looked at each other and begin to grin as they shook their heads.

"What? Oh, I get it." Katie said returning to the kitchen. "Y'all thought that I was a white girl because I'm so light-colored. Tell the truth." Katie stood with her hands on her hips with a lopsided smile on her face.

"Well, to tell you the truth sista, I knew you were one of us the minute you came into the house. Just cause you high hell a mean nothin' to me. You're a real sista in my book. Sheila now, on the other hand, was fooled through and through. But you can expect that with her ain't never been nowhere befo'." Wanda said as she reached the green beans to Katie.

"Oh, I can understand that. Plus, she is all stressed out with the baby and all due in two weeks. My that's enough to run anybody half crazy." Katie expressed. Sheila followed behind these two with a pitcher of iced tea musing over the fact that they were talking about her as is she wasn't even in the room.

"My concern is what is she goin' to do in two weeks when that baby comes? You know she still doesn't exactly know what she wanna do yet." Wanda told Katie as they both set down at the now prepared table. As Sheila set the pitcher down on the table, she looked from one woman to the other almost in shock as they continued to have a conversation about her without including her in it.

"I think we need to help her fully understand all of her options." Katie was saying. "She may even decide to keep the baby which I think would be wonderful, but of course if not then we have to help her make the right choice."
"Hello! I'm in the room with you people, dang!" Sheila cried out in exasperation.

"Sheila, you so silly, of course, you in the room. You takin' up damn ne'er half the room, that's how much you in this room!" Wanda teased.
Katie reached over to place her hand on Sheila's hand and tightly squeezed as she spoke.
"Honey, I'm so sorry for being insensitive. I just got so caught up in the conversation that Wanda and I plumb forgot all about you. I'm sorry." Katie apologized so sweetly that Sheila couldn't help but smile.

"It's okay. No harm is done. Now, let's eat. I'm starving." Sheila exclaimed.

"Me too!" Wanda put in. "Katie, you say the blessing over the food please?" Sheila asked.

"I'd be delighted," Katie answered.

As they joined hands and bowed their heads, Katie prayed to thank God not only for the food but for the newfound friendship that seemed to be growing by leaps and bounds, then the three dug into the food and began to eat and drink like there was no tomorrow. After dinner, two went back into the living room with their tea glasses in one hand and a bowl of bread pudding in the other. They talked about everything that was on each other's minds. Most of the questions were directed at Katie. She explained to them her reasoning in wanting to become a nun and she even shared her misgivings about rather or not she would go ahead and take the vow.

Wanda told how she was still angry with her parents, especially her father, for the way they treated her while she was pregnant. Sheila already knew that about Wanda already. What she didn't know was how much Wanda had begun to hate herself for not being more active in her son's life, but most of all how much she realized she enjoyed not being weighed down with the awesome responsibility of raising a child by yourself.

All this information gave Sheila a lot to think about later that night while she lay in her bed. Many tears were shed that evening and not all were sad, but all were cleansing for all three women.

"C'mon. Sheila get up it's almost time to go!" Wanda yelled as she hurriedly put on the final touches of her makeup. Sheila came dragging out of the room with her head all disheveled and still in one of Wanda's old nightgowns. None of her pajamas or little nighties fit anymore.

"Damn, I'll be glad when this shit is over," Sheila thought for the hundredth time at least. Sheila perched herself on the arm of the sofa and proceeded to yawn while she was scratched in some rather unmentionable placed.

"Stop being nasty and go wash yo' tail. We gotta go and drop ou' off to go and talk to this Mr. Tanner remember?" Sheila slouched all the way down on the couch and let out a very loud sigh.

Wanda stopped putting on the remainder of her makeup and went and sat by her cousin and began to put her arm around her to console her. Wanda remembered quite well how hard it was for her when she was pregnant.

"It's gonna be okay. We just got to trust God and try to get through these last few days. Befo' you know it, you'll have that flat belly back in no time." Wanda squeezed Sheila gently and rose from beside her. "Now, come on and get dressed. We gotta go." Wanda reminded her.

"I'm not ready," Sheila said and the tears finally begin to flow.

"I can see that woman. That's why you need to go get cleaned up and dressed." Wanda stated.

"But," Sheila continued, "I'm not ready to be a mother. I'm not strong like you. I won't be happy, not now. I just can't Wanda. I'm sorry, I'm so sorry, but I just...."

"Shhhh!!" Wanda soothed as she held Sheila in her arms as she sobbed uncontrollably. "It's all right and it's okay. Nobody's gonna force you to raise this baby. Look at me," Wanda said. "We're in this together, right?" Sheila stopped crying just long enough to nod her head.

"I'm gonna call Katie and see what we can do about puttin' you on her program." Said, Wanda

CHAPTER 6

It was pretty warm outside in the courtyard of the hospital, but under the boughs of the old oak tree, the cool breeze from the south made it quite comfortable for the three women who were sitting on the grass eating a lunch of sandwiches and soda pops. Katie, Sheila, and Wanda were now fostering.

"Sheila, if your mind is truly made up, I think this program can really be a blessing for you and the baby," Katie said.

"Do I get to see the couple who will get the baby?" Sheila asked as she stroked her stomach. "I really want this baby to have a better chance at being somebody than I can give it."

"Having second thoughts?" Wanda asked. All morning Wanda had drilled Sheila about make sure that this is what she wanted.

"No, I'm not changing my mind. I know I'm not ready to be a mother, but still want the best for the baby even if I'm not the one giving it. You or Katie put in by giving it a chance at a better life." Sheila looked form Wanda to Katie and then she lowered her head and very quietly said, "I just don't want to be condemned by God because of what I'm about to do. I need a blessing in my life, not a curse because I gave my baby away!"

Katie stared at Sheila then quickly glanced over to Wanda before she spoke. "Honey, I'm not saying that I know the reasons that God brings us through the predicaments that we face, even when we ourselves have caused it. I do know that he promises to comfort us in our times of need."

"That's right," Wanda added. "And don't the Lord say that He will open a door for us to use when we need it the most?"

Katie smiled. "Actually, it's a window that gives us a way of escape when the enemy tries to attack us. But whatever we face it will never be so great that we can't make it through. And you, missy", Katie said as she gently kissed Sheila on the cheek, "will make it through all of this. Now quit all this worrying and finish eating your lunch."

Sheila took a deep breath and said, "I know that God will watch over this baby."

"I wish He would have shined the light down on you just before you got all goofy behind that ole ass man," Wanda said.

"Girl, shut up. That's over and done with. It was good while it lasted."

"Well, look here cuz, just how good was that....?" Wanda began and then winked at Katie who was turning red.

Sheila picking up on Wanda's mood said, "Oh girl, it was sumthin' good. It was about this long and…"

"Okay, okay, okay," Katie exclaimed as she grabbed both of Sheila's hands before she could show a measurement.

Both Sheila and Wanda burst into laughter and Katie had to join in. They finished eating, and then Katie and Wanda helped Sheila up. They all walked into the hospital where Sheila finished filling out the final forms for the program. The search for parents would now begin.

CHAPTER 7

The clock in the living room read 3:30 pm. Janice Jacobs smiled as she tossed her purse on the sofa and walked into the kitchen to take out a pack of turkey necks from the freezer. Dinner would not only be early this evening but she had a surprise to share with her husband when he got in from work. She'd stopped at the post office on her way from work and along with a couple of bills, a sales paper from Western Auto and a copy of the latest issue of Life magazine was a letter from the Office of Family Services in New Orleans.

"This has to be it." She said to herself. "Lord, please let it be it!" she whispered.

The letter began as usual with the normal opening:

> Dear Mr. and Mrs. Jacobs,
>
> We are pleased to inform you that your file has been selected and after review, we would like to invite you to a formal interview here at our New Orleans office. Please be advised that this is not an official adoption notice, but preparation for what could very well become one. Your appointment is scheduled for 9:30 am, Tuesday, 8-22-1967. We look forward to seeing you then.
>
> Sincerely,
Sis. Katie Wells
Asst. Director of Child Placement Services

I KNOW A BLESSING WHEN I SEE ONE

Janice felt like shouting for joy when she finished reading the letter. She'd just told her sister Sue on the phone the night before that she hoped that the program that they'd been referred to would not dismiss their application like the other two agencies did earlier. They informed her that although she and her husband met all the requirements to be adoptive parents, they were being turned down due to their ages.

"Janice, don't let them people get you down." Sue had said. "It is God's will you and Clay are gonna get a child. As they say, He may not come when you want Him to but He's always right on time."

Janice smiled at herself remembering the conversation between her and Susan. She and her husband James had one son, but after some severe complications, Sue could no longer have children. Three years earlier they had been chosen by one of the same agencies, that had turned she and Clay down, to adopt their own child. So now, they had two boys in their home. Janice's attention came back to the matter at hand and finished cutting some onions and peppers up to season the turkey necks. She wanted everything to be just right. Her news was exciting, but could she convince Clay to take Saturday off from work at the mill in order to go to the interview with her. He really hated the fact that they didn't have any children of their own and Janice knew all too well. Yet, Clay never gave any sign of resentment or misgivings towards her. After 20 years of marriage, they were still in love with each other.

Supper was almost ready now and she took the bread pudding out of the oven and set it on the counter to cool when the telephone ran.

"Hello," Janice said in a not so usual singing tone.

"Girl, you sound mighty happy. What's going on down there?" It was Janice's oldest sister Lea. She about an hour's drive from town in Opelousas and usually called twice a week to talk to Janice.

"Hey Girl," Janice said as she took off her apron and started to prim her hair in the ball mirror. "I can't talk too long. Clay will be here in a few minutes and I need to set the table."

"Set the table?" Lea asked. "What's going on over there that I don't know about?" Janice laughed at her sister's nosey attitude. She has been like that since they were kids. Now they were grown, middle-aged and Lea was still all up in bother younger sister's business.

"My business and not yours!" Janice responded.

"Girl, your business ain't that much worth talkin' bout anyway. I'm just tryin' to make you feel good 'cause I know you are bored stiff out there in the sticks." Lea retorted.

That was Lea. Always picking and teasing her sisters about their lives when in fact she was quite lonely. Ever since her husband died, her only social avenues were the church, which she wasn't as attentive as she used to be, and her sisters Janice and Sue who were both well aware of how empty the oldest sister's life had indeed become. So, they endured a lot of her rudeness and her antics as the family busy-body.

"When you and clay coming down here anyway? I thought y'all was coming last weekend?" Lea asked.

"Clay been working on Saturday for the past three weekends, but it's supposed to slow up soon," Janice responded. "Besides, the extra money is always a blessing."

"Child, I know that's right. Well just thank God for what He's providing right now. How's teaching coming along?" Lea said.

"It's been great. The kids are pretty good and it helps that the school is Catholic plus it's only a 10-mile drive to work so it works out fine for us." Janice explained.

"Well, I'm glad it's working out. Now, back to what I asked you to begin with." Lea said.

"Lord, this woman just won't quit!" exclaimed Janice.

"Damn right, now, what's going on?" Lea asked.

"Well, if you must know, I heard from another agency and they want me and Clay to come down to interview next week. Isn't that great!?" Janice explained.

There was a brief pause and then Lea said, "Oh, a course that's great, but I don't want you to get your hopes up too high. Remember what happened in the last couple of times."

"It'll be different this time. God is on our side. You'll see." Janice said.

"I hope so, honey. I really do. Well for once, I'm gonna let you go do whatever you gotta do. Let me know what happens. Bye girl."

"Bye sis." And Janice hung up and went back to the kitchen.

CHAPTER 8

Janice glanced at her watch again and re-crossed her legs as she tried to get comfortable in the waiting area of the Family Support Program of Sacred Heart Charity Hospital.

"Woman will you hold still!?" Clay said. "You act like something done crawled up the back of yo' dress and just won't stop bitin'!"

Janice rolled her eyes at Clay as he sat there next to her. "Look at him," she thought, "Sittin' there like he ain't got a care in the world! He doesn't even realize how serious this is. This very well could be our last chance."

"Clay, do you know how important this is? We may not get another case."

"Listen, Janice, if the Lord wants us to raise another child, it will happen. So, stop worrying!" Clay exclaimed.

"I don't wanna raise any more foster children. We have done that for the past 15 years. I want my own baby, period!" Janice stressed.

"You not gon' get nothing if you sit here and worry yo'self into a heart attack. Besides, we can't rush the process go faster so you might as well rest yo' nerves because you getting' on mine!" Clay retorted. Then with a smile, he pinched Janice. She swatted at him as he rose from his seat and reached into his shirt pocket and pulled out his cigarettes. "I'm going outside to stretch my legs and have a smoke." Clay said. "I'll be back in a few minutes."

"Don't be gone too long. They might call while you outside." Janice responded.

"Don't worry. I won't take long." He bent down and kissed Janice on the lips and he was a bit surprised that she didn't turn her cheek for him to kiss instead. She didn't like to smudge her lipstick.

"Give me some gum before you go," Janice asked. Clay reached into his pants pocket and pulled out a pack of Doublemint gum and gave his wife a slice.

"Damn". He thought as he walked down the hall. She must be mighty nervous.

Janice continued to fidget from one thing to another as she waited for their appointment. The clock on the wall reached 9:40 am and her watch read the exact same thing. She opened the gum wrapper and popped the stick of gum in her mouth and within a minute she was popping it for all it was worth. She got up and got a magazine off the table and flipped through it, not really looking at anything. She'd like reading life magazine, but on today she just couldn't on anything else other than the impending meeting. Janice tossed the magazine back on the table and began to pace back and forth as she popped her gum.

"Woman, stop poppin' that gum in here. Your actin' worse than them chaps you been teaching." Clay exclaimed.

"I feel like I'm about to pop! What's taking them so long. If they don't want us, Clay, I just don't know what I'm gone do." Janice said. Her mind was beginning to grab hold of some very negative thoughts when Clay took her into his embrace and then walked her back to the chair.

"Don't worry baby, that door is gonna open any minute. Just watch." Clay said. He smiled that crooked smile at her that always warmed her heart and she even giggled. She was about to speak when the door to the office abruptly opened and a young woman dressed up like a num (but in Janice's opinion was too young to be one) breezed into the room with a smile as bright as a 100-watt bulb.

"Good morning," Katie said. 'I'm sister Katie Wells, and I'll be handling your interview this morning. Won't you please come in?" As Katie ushered in Clay and Janice, she continued to chatter. "I'm sorry you had to wait, but there were some matters that I needed to attend to that were of the utmost importance," Katie explained.

"We understand, and we appreciate you taking time out to interview us," Janice replied.

"Oh, it's my pleasure, but please sit down and make yourselves as comfortable as you can," Katie said. "Now, let's see, ah yes. Mr. and Mrs. Jacobs." Katie spoke as she began to flip through the file that she had retrieved from a stack of plain tan ones. Janice wondered if that whole stack were people who were waiting to be interviewed or those who had already been interviewed? She wondered what was she and Clay's odds of being chosen this time. She sighed and even slumped a little in her chair. Clay reached over and gently squeezed her hand to reassure.

"I must see. I've been conducting interviews for the past few days, and your folder has truly impressed me. It says here that you've actually been foster parents on two separate occasions raising both sets, from kids to young adults."

Janice sat up and simply said, "Well, it wasn't easy but God provided us to be a blessing for them."

"Truly God is moving on behalf of His children." Responded Katie. "I was looking through your files and I see that you actually were able to meet the requirements in order to adopt but for reasons unexplained on the application you weren't accepted. Would you mind discussing those issues?"

"Well," Clay began, "when we first applied, oh, about 15 years ago, we were turned down because we didn't make enough money."

Janice spoke, "What my husband means is that there were a couple of other families that were financially better off than we were at the time."

"I see," Katie said. "So, how are things now, financially speaking?"

"Oh, it's a lot better. We own our home and we both work but if we were to be selected, I would take a leave of absence to care for the baby."

"Wouldn't that be a problem, Mrs. Jacobs" Katie asked.

"Oh, no!" Janice said. "I'm a teacher and I would still receive pay because it would be considered medical leave."

"That would be great, Mrs. Jacobs. Isn't that a Catholic school you work for?" Katie asked.

"Yes, as you can see on my application that I've been working there for the past five years."

"Okay, well it seems that you are definitely ready for our program. You are financially stable and everything else seems to be in order. Just one last question. Do you think your ages will be a problem raising a child for the next 18 years?" Katie waited for their responses because unlike the other agencies, she wanted to know from these people who she believed were perfect for giving Sheila's baby a chance could indeed be active parents in the child's life.

"Sister, if you have someone else who's more qualified to have this child just say so." Clay began. "We've been turned down twice as you already know because of our ages. But with our age come a lot of experience and wisdom, a lot more than your average young couple has to give."

Clay uncrossed his legs and began to rise from the chair when Janice grabbed his hand and said, "Wait!"

Clay looked down in the pleading eyes of his wife. He knew that this was probably their last chance to adopt and he knew how much she wanted her own child. He remembered how she'd cried and even prayed that God would heal her so she could have had children of her own, but that hadn't happened. He'd seen how she had hurt when the last agency turned them down. "Lord, if you don't want us to have this child, then please help Janice accept it and move on." Clay prayed in his heart.

"Mr. Jacobs, I really do think that you and your wife would be the best fit for the child," Katie explained.

"Sister Katie, Janice said through trembling lips. "I've lost three children in my lifetime. Three times I had joy only to be crushed." She could not hold back her tears any longer. "I hoped three times only left to feel hopeless. This child is my last hope! I'm not too old, and just because I was barren does not mean I can't be a good mother. That child would be my blessing!"

"I'm sorry for upsetting you, Janice," Katie said through her tears. "But I just had to know for myself." She flashed back in her mind recalling al of her previous conversations with Sheila and Wanda. She especially recalled the conversation between her and Sheila on that picnic lunch. She knew that even though Sheila had accepted the fact that she wasn't ready to be a full-fledged mother, she still wanted to make sure the baby would get better than what she could have offered. She'd promised them and herself that she would do her best to find the best couple to parent Sheila's child. She looked at this middle-aged couple who lived at least two hours from the city in a rural area. She was the love they had for each other, Clay's protective nature for Janice and knew he'd be a strong father and as for Janice, well she had won her over from the very beginning.

"We'll be in touch with you," Katie said as she stood up and ushered them out. "Thank you again and God bless."

As they walked through the door, Janice whispered to Clay saying, "Well, that went well. Like you always say, honey, my big moth will one day get me into something I can't get out of. Look like that day has arrived."

"Baby, don't worry yourself over nothing. I'm glad that you said it." Clay stopped and turned Janice to face him looking into her eyes he said, "Baby, your words were not only how you feel, but you told her how I feel too. I know I'm just a regular ol' hand but I'm glad God gave me you."

"That's because nobody else would have put up with me," Janice said with a smile. I love you ol' man." Janice said with a smile.

"I love you too baby," Clay responded. "Now, let's get outta here and get us something to eat."

Just then the door opened and Katie came out with Janice's purse. "Janice, you left things a woman can't be without." Katie teased.

"Oh, my, I hadn't noticed. Thank you so much." Janice said as Katie reached her purse. They paused, then suddenly and unexplainably embraced. When they released each other, a decision had been made.

CHAPTER 9

Sheila felt like she was about to burst. She walked slowly back into the bathroom to look at herself again in the full-length mirror on the back of the bathroom door. As she lifted her blouse and turned sideways to examine her stomach, she gasped at the size of her stomach and the seemingly ever-increasing stretch marks that were all over her.

"Damn, they're everywhere," Sheila said to herself. "At this rate, it will take all the cocoa butter and all the coconuts in all of Hawaii to get rid of these."

She passed her hand over the lower portion of her belly on down to where her unbuttoned shorts began. All she could do was shake her head from side to side and swear under her breath. Then she had an urge to pee again so she stretched her blouse over her stomach and stepped over to the toilet. She dropped her shorts, set down and proceeding to let out what she considered a tank full of water. Just as she was finished, the telephone rang.

She heard when Wanda answered, "Hello. Hey, Katie, whatcha doing? She right here, you need to talk to her? Hold on. Sheila, telephone!"

"I'm coming", Sheila responded. "Who is it?" Sheila asked as she walked into the living room.

"It's Katie," Wanda answered and reached Sheila the receiver.

"Hey, girl, what's shaking?" Sheila asked. The formalities between them had completely faded away and she and Wanda looked at Katie as just another member of the family.

"Hey, Sheila. I was just calling to let you know that I finished all the interviews yesterday!"

"Really? That fast, wow! Well, what's next?" Sheila asked.

"I need to go over everything with the Reverend Mother first, of course, but I really want to come by later and tell you about some of the couples who came to apply. Will you have time this afternoon?" Katie asked.

"Sure, come around at two," Sheila said.

"Any progress?" Wanda asked.

"I think so," Sheila responded. "Katie says she's coming over later this afternoon to tell us about some of the people who've applied to take my baby." Sheila sat on the couch and lovingly patted her belly.

"Wanda walked over and sat beside her. "Sheila, I want you to listen and really think about what I'm about to say." Wanda began. "Ever since you first found out that you were pregnant, the only thing that you allowed yourself to think was how you couldn't have this baby and how bad it would mess up your life."

"I know and I know sometimes I get on your nerves." Sheila began to explain.

"That's not what I'm concerned about. You've always said everything about not keeping your baby, but it's as if all of a sudden you're starting to have second thoughts." When Wanda saw that her cousin was really listening, she took a deep breath and continued. "Sheila, times are hard and the way it is for us black folks, hell, I don't know if it's ever gonna get any better. So, I can't and don't blame you for wanting this child to get a better chance in life." Wanda reached over and grabbed her cousin's hand and said, "But if you want to keep your baby, then that's what you should do. Nobody is gonna force you one way or the other."

Sheila knew that her tears would start flowing at any moment. "It's just that sometimes I really wonder what it would be like to keep my baby. I mean it's still my baby until I actually give it up, right?" Sheila asked.

"Oh, course it's your baby and ain't nobody gonna take it from you if you want to keep it!" Wanda said with such determination that she made Sheila smile. "We will make it and we can take care of both of our children together."

"Well, Katie will be here later, so we'll talk then," Sheila said.

Katie rushed through the halls of the hospital. She knew her training had to be perfect in order to catch the Reverend Mother between her morning rounds and pre-noon summary. She thought to herself about the last meeting they had regarding the program. She'd submitted a couple's file earlier along with the Jacobs' file. She heavily favored the Jacobs and she believed that the Reverend Mother was also leaning towards them as well. She turned the corner and also ran into one of the doctors.

"Oh, I'm so sorry." She apologized.

"No problem." The doctor replied. "But what's the hurry sister?"

"I have to catch the Reverend Mother before she leaves for the lecture or I'll have to wait until tomorrow."

"Well, you don't need to hurry, because her assistant was on her way to meet her." He replied.

"Thank you, and sorry again," Katie yelled over her shoulder as she turned the next corner.

The Reverend Mother was standing in the outer entrance to her office, talking to her assistant. She looked up and noticed Katie jester for her to come in. As Katie entered, the Reverend Mother whispered some instructions to her assistants who nodded and with a smile as greeting to Katie, she hurried off on some errand.

"Please, come in my dear." Said the Reverend Mother. "I was hoping to see you before I went to the lecture. Please, sit down." As Katie took her seat, Reverend Mother continued. "I've been keeping track of this new program and progress you've been making. I think you have been doing a wonderful job this far and your selections are outstanding." Katie smiled. It was rare that anyone got a compliment from Reverend Mother. She was always so strict and rigid. Some even viewed her like a mother hen brooding over her chicks. But that was her way.

"Thank you, Mother." Katie began. "Truly the Lord is leading these people to us that we may find the right couple to parent these children."

"Quite right, my dear." Replied Reverend Mother. "Our duty in this matter is quite clear in that we must do our best to make sure that the safety of these children is provided for in the best possible way." She paused for a moment for Katie to reply, but after an awkward moment of silence, she continued. "Now, I've been looking at the files of some of the families that have applied, especially that last three you've narrowed it down to."

This set Katie aback. She was told that this project, even though it was a test mode, was her program and she had the final choice in the selection of the couples. Now she had an aching feeling that after she'd done all the leg work, the Reverend Mother was about to pull rank and make the final decision without as so much taking time to interview not even one couple.

"I see here that you did one extensive amount of research and by doing such a thorough job, I feel honored to be a part of this selection process." She said.

"Thank you, Mother, if I may...." Katie began but was cut off abruptly.

"So, I've taken the liberty to select this nice young couple from Alexandria, uh the James family. They're both young and vibrant with stable income and a strong background in the church." Reverend Mother pronounced as the pushed the file across the desk to Katie.

Katie looked up and was about to protest when she saw that indeed the look in the Reverend Mother's eyes and slight smile (or was that a smirk) left no room for discussion.

"I shall be in contact with the James family in a day or so to share with them the good news." She said. "Please notify the other couples that we are sorry, but they just didn't quite fit the bill." With that, she rose and walked around her desk reaching the other two folders to Katie. "Now, I must be going. Do be a dear and keep me posted on the condition of the expecting mother."

"Yes, ma'am." Was all Katie could muster. She took the folders from the Reverend and hesitated for just long enough for Reverend Mother to notice.

"Is there anything wrong, my dear?" she asked.

Katie took a deep breath and plunged in. "Mother the James family is a nice choice, but I truly feel that the Jacobs are much more suitable for this child. I've met with them and they have so much to offer. Any child would be double blessed to have them as parents."

"Yet, they are no longer you and well into middle age." Reverend Mother replied. "I believe it would be too stressful at their ages to raise a newborn. Plus, the fact that James is Catholic and I for one, would prefer to see the child raised as Catholic." She concluded. "Now, if there's nothing further, I really must be going. Have a wonderful day child." She patted Katie on the back as she ushered her out of her office and into the hall.

"You have a great day too, Mother," Katie said as she walked off. Not in any way trying to disguise the disapproval in her voice.

She walked slowly back to her office to try to figure out what was she going to tell the other two families. She could see Janice Jacobs in her mind and she knew that no matter what the Reverend Mother said the right choice would be Janice and Clayton. She'd talked to James' family and in their interview, they came across as cold and distant. They were not the ones for Sheila's baby and if ever she wished that Sheila would change her mind, now would be the time. She walked into her office, dropped the folders and put her head down on her desk. This day was not starting as she planned. There was a knock at the door. Katie jumped up startled as she looked around her office and out the window. It was getting dark outside. Katie jerked herself up from her desk and looked at the clock on the wall.

"My God," Katie thought, "I must've fallen asleep." The knock resumed at the door and she began to move towards the outer office and smoothed her dress against her thighs as she walked. Katie reached for the handle and began to say, "I'm sorry, but we're not…"

But before she could finish the sentence Wanda finished it for her saying, "Opened at this time, please come back and see us tomorrow." Then she and Sheila said together mimicking their friend, "Be blessed in Jesus' name."

All Katie could do was smile at her two friends, friends who she had come to love like sisters. She looked at them both and opened her arms as she walked to take them into her embrace, needing the comfort of their presence.

"Hey, girl. What's wrong with you?" Wanda asked. They all sat in the outer office. Sheila sat next to Katie while Wanda sat across. Sheila took one good look at Katie and knew that she was fretting about something.

"What's wrong love?" Sheila asked as she placed her arm gently around Katie.

"It's all this ripping and running she doing trying to please everybody." Wanda put in.

"It's been a really stressful day," Katie said. She leaned against Sheila letting her head rest on her shoulder.

"You've had these types of days before and never have you let it get you down like this," Sheila said. "So, what's going on?"

"It's probably that other nun that I see you having to run and jump every time she so much as bat her eyes," Wanda added. "Girl, you let that woman put too much pressure on you for no reason."

"I don't want to talk about her but I am sorry for not making it over this afternoon." Katie apologized. "I was just exhausted."

"We understand," Sheila said. "Hell, I feel tired all the time. I feel like I'm on a full-time job with overtime toting this baby."

"Girl, stop. It's almost over and before you know it, you'll really be tired having to work part-time, take a course or two at the college and deal with that chap." Wanda put in.

This comment brought Katie out of her daze. "Excuse me, what did you say Wanda?" Katie asked.

"What part? You mean the part about taking courses at the college or working part-time." Wanda said.

Sheila joined in. "She's asking about the part concerning the baby, right?" Katie slowly nodded her head.

"Well, that's what we came over here to talk to you about." She continued. "Wanda has been talking and I've been doing some thinking and well, maybe I could keep the baby and still make it. I mean, I know it's gonna be rough and all but…." Before Sheila could finish her sentence, Katie grabbed her in an embrace and gently squeezed. When she finally let go, Katie simply said to Sheila, "Thank God!" Sheila was so taken aback that she backed herself up at arm's length to place some space between them.

Wanda leaned in and asked, "Katie did we hear you right?"

Katie, who from the moment Sheila told her, had covered her face. Now she removed them realizing that she had started to shed tears due to her relief. She hadn't realized that she was so stressed out up until that moment. Now, she really felt relief. "I know it might not seem to make sense with everything I was trying to get done for the adoption of the baby." Katie began.

"And I want you to know that I appreciate everything you did for me." Sheila put in. I'm sorry I put you through all the anguish."

"The important thing is that you've decided to keep the baby." Katie proclaimed. "Now we can all get ready for its arrival."

"So, you're okay?" Wanda asked.

"Great!" was Katie's response.

"Good. Let's all go home then."

"Oh Lord, I'm glad that's over," Sheila said. "I thought we were going to go a couple of rounds with you, because of all the work you've done."

Katie stared at Sheila with a look of disbelief which in turn made Sheila cringe. "Well," Sheila begins, "you can never tell sometimes right?!"

Katie spoke, "Girl, you should have known me better than that by now. It's not about me, my programs or anything like that. All I want is to see you happy and what's best for the baby."

"I believe that's what we all want," Wanda said as she got up. "You coming with us Katie?"

"I'll be down in a couple of minutes. I have to make a telephone call." Katie said.

"You want us to wait?" Sheila asked as she followed Wanda to the door.

"No. You two go on ahead. This won't take long." And Katie hurried back into her office and sat down opening the James' file. She hesitated for a moment then dialed the number. She let the phone ring several times and was about to hand up when someone picked up.

"James residence." A woman's voice said.

Katie paused for a moment as she pictured the face of Mrs. James. Katie remembered how she made her feel when she first met her. She was a school teacher that gave off the impression that she was very reserved, prim and proper. Katie could not picture a baby being nurtured by such a woman.

"Hello?" the voice said.

This snapped Katie out of her thoughts. "Mrs. James?" she asked. "Good evening. This is sister Katie Wells at Sacred Heart Charity Hospital and I'm calling about the adoption process."

"Is the child read?" Mrs. James asked.

God, she sounds so cold Katie thought. "No, ma'am. The mother has decided to raise her child."

"I see." Mrs. James began. "Is there anything else available?" She asked.

"No. Not at this time." Katie responded. "But we will be in contact with you when an opportunity comes up."

"I'm sure you will. Goodbye." Said, Mrs. James.

Katie just stared at the receiver not believing how cold this last conversation was. "God thank you for not letting this adoption go through! She's terrible!" Katie thought to herself.

She closed the folder, got up and filed it back into the file cabinet. She put them under those who had been rejected. They were definitely not what any child needed no matter what they had to offer. Then she walked back to her desk and began to open the Jacobs file. She hated to have to call them with any news other than having a baby ready for them.

"These are the ones that would make any child happy." She thought. "God." Katie said as she picked up the phone to dial the number." Thy will be done."

"Katie!" Wanda yelled. "Come on here girl. We are waiting for you, remember? This stuff can wait 'till tomorrow." Katie put the phone down, grabbed her things and closed the door on her way out.

CHAPTER 10

The twelve-noon whistle had just blown and Clay was already in his Pontiac Starchief on his way to meet Janice at the café for lunch. She hadn't gone to work today and they had made plans to have lunch together, and he didn't want to be late. She would have the food already ordered and probably waiting at the table knowing that they only had half an hour.

"Hey Clay. Hold up. You going to the café?"

"Come on, Daddy B. I'm gonna be late," Clay said as he gunned the engine. Daddy B jumped in the car and shook a camel to smoke.

"Thank you."

"What you and Jean doing tonight?" asked Clay.

"Much of nothin'!" Daddy B answered. "Junior has been sick with the flu so she and I gonn' jus' stay at home and watch T.V."

"Ain't nothin' wrong with that." Clay said.

"I tell you what though", Daddy B began, "I wish he was well, so, you and I could take a trip down to the city again. Hot damn! We had some fun down there! Say whatever happened to that fine pretty young girl that you were messin' with?"

Clay looked at his friend as he pulled into the parking lot of the café. "Look, didn't I tell you to forget about them gals?" Clay said.

"Yeah, yeah, yeah you said that befo', but you can't sit there and tell me that you don't miss ridin' that pretty young piece of a...." Daddy B replied.

Before he could finish, Clay cut him off. "Listen up B, that was a mistake. I shouldn't get with that girl, to begin with." Clay said.

"I almost lost Janice behind that foolish gal. Besides, I shoulda been stopped that whole thing."

"You ain't never heard nothin' since then?" asked Daddy B.

"No, and I'm glad." Clay said. "It's better all da way round. Now let's go inside."

"Hey, baby," Janice said as Clay walked up to her and kissed her. "I was wondering if you be able to make it or not?" Janice waved at the waitress behind the counter and went on talking to her husband. "I knew the time would be tight so I ordered you a large hamburger and fries. That's okay?" Janice asked, but she already knew Clay's answer. They had been together so long they could practically read each other's minds. "Why couldn't I read his mind last year when he kept going to New Orleans?" she asked herself. "Stop it girl. Whatever that was it's over!" she told herself. She looked at Clayton and it still was amazing to her, how a man his age could still attract so many women. She remembered how it was like a battle with all the other women to see who would win the prize. She'd won his love even without having to spread her legs first to do it. Clay was an honorable man, but could easily have been a pimp with the right push from the wrong people. She remembered how he and his cousins would stroll down Canal Street on Saturday nights. They were all light-skinned with their hair so wavy you could get seasick looking at them. She thought all these thoughts in a matter of moments as she reached across the table they were sitting at and ran her fingers through his now graying, yet still wavy hair. She smiled as she thought, "Yeah, whatever was going on, it's over and I'm still the one."

"What's going through that head of yours, woman?" Clay asked. The waitress set their food in front of them and walked away.

"Clayton Jacobs", Janice began, "do you still love me the way you used to?" Even as she said it, fear flooded her heart not truly knowing what Clay's response would be.

Clay looked up from the food. He knew from the look in Janice's eyes that his answer was critical. He took a swallow of the royal crown cola he was drinking to help swallow the food and to buy time to quickly put the right words together.

"Janice", he said, "we've been together for a very long time. We did have some ups and downs, and I ain't gone sit here and lie and say that everything has been great." He let that settle in and continued. "You did say in the past that God and His mercy is what brought us this far." Janice was about to say something but Clay put his hand over his lips indicating that he wasn't finished. "To answer your question, No, I don't love you like I used to, but I do love you better." Clay said. Janice looked bewildered but remained silent. "I love you better because I know you better and you know me better. We've been through hell and high water together and are the better for it, and every day that we wake up together we get better and better." The tears welled up in her eyes and all she wanted to do was reach over that table and hold her husband forever.

He looked at her and smiled that crooked smile and said, "Now stop all that crying befo' that black stuff gets to running everywhere and have you looking like a raccoon!" Clay said.

Janice popped Clay and started to laugh a little. Then she got up to go to the ladies' room to check her makeup. She bent and kissed Clay on the ear and walked off. Clay peeped over his shoulder and smiled to himself. Yeah, he knew he had a good thing in Janice and she was in his opinion worth her weight in gold.

"To think I almost threw all this away for a piece of young tail." He thought.

Just then Daddy B passed by on his way to the counter, then turned around and said, "I remember now!" he said to Clay.

"Remember what B?" Clay responded.

"The names of the girls in the city, Wanda and Sheila." He exclaimed.

Clay gave Daddy B a look that could have curdled milk. He jumped up and pulled his friend down in the chair where Janice had just left. "Listen, fool," Clay begins, "are you tryin' to get all this shit started again between me and Janice!? You know how rough it was last year. You barely got back in with Jean when all that mess came out!" Before Daddy B could say a word, Clay continued. "Look, from now on I don't want to hear another word from you about what happened or any talk about the two you hear?" Clay said with a rumble in his throat. He was a slow man to anger, but when he did, look out!

Daddy B said, "Whoa now Clay. I ain't mean no harm. I was just funnin' with cha'. Besides, Jean's in the washroom with Janice anyway. I wouldn't say anything around either one of them. Do you think I want my head on the chopping block with Jean holding the axe? Besides, for all we know, the gals are probably back in Mississippi or wherever they come from."

"Yeah, well just be more careful from now on." Clay said. He settled back into his seat and began to wolf down the rest of his food. At that same moment, laughter was heard as Jean and Janice returned to the dining area.

"Hey Clay. How ya' doing?" Jean blurted out. She was a big black woman with some of the prettiest brown eyes you ever saw. She and Janice were best buddies. Since Janice loved kids and Jean and Daddy B had a house full of them, Janice was always available as a last-minute baby sitter.

"I'm hanging in there, Jean." Clay replied through a mouth full of French fries.

"Clay, slow down baby before you choke yourself." Janice chided in.

"Sorry baby, but I gotta hurry and get back to work. Man, look at the time." Clay said as he jumped up and wrapped up the leftovers of his hamburgers and tucked it in his lunchbox. "I'll see you when I get home." He bent over and kissed her on the cheek and headed for the door as Daddy B released Jean and hurried after.

As the two climbed into the car they began to talk about the events of the current happenings. Daddy B kept going on and on about Jean and the children and about how the prices of food and clothing were going up.

"Man, I just can't seem to get my head above water, Clay." He said. "Every time I turn around, I'm having to buy this or fix this and pay for that. I just can't get a break!"

"Well, ain't nobody told you to keep on poppin' all them children in Jean. You see how she is. Hell, if you breathe on her he wrong way she gets pregnant." Clay said.

"Well, I hope things start to get better soon. It's been so long that I had a paycheck to myself that I almost forgot what it is to have my own money." Daddy B said.

"Don't worry. Like Janice always say, trouble don't last always. Just hold on, your blessing coming!" said Clay

"Well, I sure hope it hurry up and get here. Say, speaking of children ain't you and Janice supposed to be getting a baby soon?" Daddy B asked.

Clay turned into the parking lot of the mill and killed the engine. "Yeah, we still tryin'." Clay began. "Things seem to be looking pretty good. We went to a meeting last week to talk to the lady over the program."

"Where'd y'all go, Alexandria?" Daddy B asked as both men got out of the car and briskly walked back to the front office to clock back in.

Clay hesitated and then answered, "Nah, we went to New Orleans Charity Hospital. They got a new program that the nuns are runnin'."

"Man, you should have told me you were going back down there. Hell. Me, you, Jean and Janice coulda went together." Daddy B said as he punched in. "Then we could have left them there while we went over to see if them gals were around somewhere. Hell, that would have been worth the trip." He said.

"You just don't get it do you, man?" Clay said. "What we did, no what I did down there was wrong and I ain't gone make the same mistake twice." Clay punched in and walked through the entrance and headed to his drop.

"Now hold on a minute, Clay. You mean to tell me you not the least bit interested in seeing that girl Sheila again? Hell, she was crazy behind you." Daddy B said.

"That's one of the main problems. Can't you see?" Clay said as he slowed down to a standstill to finish this conversation. "She acts like I was her husband and all! I might have been mad with Janice for a while; even long enough to hook up with the girl, but I wasn't ever planning to leave Janice for that child. Now if you want to go back down and get back with the other one and ear up to your whole life, then that's yo' business, but leave me out!" Clay walked off and went to his work area.

CHAPTER 11

Sheila yawned as she watched the credits roll down the television screen. The movie she'd been watching hadn't been much to her liking but here was nothing else to do. It was unbelievable hot and the fans were only blowing hot air. She looked at the phone on the stand and wondered who she could call at this time of the day. "Nobody in their right mind wants to be out in this heat." She said to herself. She pushed herself up from the couch and wobbled to the kitchen for lemonade. She looked at the calendar and it was the 28th of August. "Any minute now and you'll be free." She said to her stomach as she opened the icebox. She took the lemonade out of the Frigidaire and set it on the counter. Then she got a glass and then tool the ice tray out of the freezer pat and pulled the lever so the ice would fall out. Sheila put several cubes in her glass and then turned the faucet on to re-fill the tray with water and rinsed her ice off.

After she put the tray back in the freezer, she poured herself a glass of lemonade and put the pitcher back in the icebox. Sheila hated moments like this because it gave her time to think. She'd always chided herself for being rash and impatient. Now that she had time to think about keeping the baby, she was faced with the reality that she was completely unprepared to raise this child. The fact was that she'd gone through her entire pregnancy with the idea of giving the baby up for adoption. But now, right at the end, she had absolutely nothing. No clothes for the baby, no vouchers and no money coming in.

"What the hell was I thinking!" she said to herself. She knew that since she couldn't work anymore the burden was on Wanda and hat was a big enough strain by itself. "What if the baby gets sick or needs special attention?" she thought. "I can't even afford to take care of myself." She placed her hand on her stomach and said aloud, "The only thing I can offer you is my love." She walked with her glass to go sit back down, but decided to g and sit on the porch instead. Even as she opened the screen door, a little breeze caressed her face inviting her to come outside. Once she got outside and began to really look at the neighborhood in a way that she never had before. Sheila watched as some of the men stood on the corner doing nothing. "Just wasting away." She thought with disgust. She looked at the women and girls in the neighborhood who had children and were relying on the state welfare program to survive. They were there; uneducated, and falling hopelessly prey to the stigma of being poor, ignorant and black with no apparent end in sight. Then she focused on the children themselves. Children of all ages were around the neighborhood. They were running wild and unkempt. Some half-naked, others dirty from playing in the streets all day. She watched some of the older girls in their teens smiling up in some of the lanky teenage boys' faces completely taken in by them. Others toting babies on their hips that either belonged to their mothers, sisters or themselves. All of them living as if this form of lifestyle was all there was to it. Sheila was all too familiar with it. She left it behind in Mississippi only to find it even in greater numbers in the city. The air was stuff and it was so hot that it was hard to breathe. "Is this what you want your baby to call home, Sheila?" she asked herself. "No. I love you enough to give you better than what I have to offer, which is nothing." Sheila stood and walked back into the house and picked up the phone and called Katie. After the third ring, Katie answered.

"Hello, Katie. I know you're probably busy, but I really need to talk to you." Sheila said with a rush of words.

"Sure sweetie, but I can't come over now, but I'll try to get there this evening. What's this all about?" Katie asked. She could hear the anxiety in Sheila's voice.

"It's concerning the well-being and future of my baby. Look, I can be over at your office in about fifteen minutes." She said as she reached for her purse on the living room table.

"Okay, but you sure that won't put too much of a strain on you with you being so close to your due date?" Katie asked.

"I'm pregnant Katie, I'm not crippled. I'll see you in fifteen minutes, ya hear?" was Sheila's response.

"Then I'll be here waiting. See you in a little while. Bye." Katie said and hung up. Sheila hung up the receiver, looked at herself in the hall mirror and decided she was okay and left the house.

Katie sat in her chair wondering what was going on with Sheila that would cause her to drop everything to come to talk to her. She hoped nothing bad had happened or anything out of the ordinary. But she didn't have time to contemplate what was on Sheila's mind. She'd know soon enough. She looked at the different folders of applicants who had hoped to have become adoptive parents. She sighed and began to jot information down out of each file for future references before storing them back into the active file cabinet. She was working on the last one when she heard Sheila's voice and she waved her to come in and have a seat.

"So, what's up girl. You sounded as if you had an emergency." Katie asked.

"I did. I got pregnant and I want the best for this baby." Sheila said.

"We both knew that. Now, what's wrong, Sheila?" Katie asked. Just then the phone rang and Katie dropped the file card she had in her hand as she answered the telephone.

Sheila for some reason felt curious. She scooted up in the chair to get a better look. She already knew that Katie had been working on updating the files for her adoption program and she only hoped she hadn't called the ones she had decided on to let them now that her baby was longer available. In fact, as far as she was concerned, not only was she willing to place her child into an adoptive couple's arms, but she even wished she could have done the interviews along with Katie. On the card at the top were written in red ink these words: Best Couple Available. Then what Sheila read after that set things into motion that would change things forever. She shuttered and with trembling fingers picked up the card and read the names of the couple. There is was clear as day. Katie had hung up and was looking up at Sheila who was now crying.

"What's wrong?" she asked as she moved around to Sheila's side. The card read Clayton and Janice Jacobs.

"That's my baby's father!" Sheila whispered and dropped the card.

Katie's eyes widened as she stared at Sheila, who seemed to be in a state of shock. She couldn't believe she heard her friend's right. It just didn't add up.... or did it? She began to think about all the past conversations that they'd had along with Wanda. She recalled them mentioning some of their wild nights out on the town. She even suspected that Wanda, though she may not have actually been there, knew full well who the father of Sheila's baby was. But Mr. Jacobs? Janice's clean-cut and seemingly trustworthy husband? Wow! Maybe she didn't have such a great judge of character as she thought. Maybe she should leave the decision making in the hands of the Reverend Mother. "After all she has years of experience doesn't, she?" Katie thought as her mind whirled. Katie snapped back into the now when the sounds of Sheila sobbing became apparent. She placed her arm around Sheila and spoke.

"Honey, are you saying that this man that I interviewed is the father of your child?" Katie asked.

Sheila reached into her purse fumbling for something while Katie grabbed some tissue for her. As she reached the tissue to Sheila, she watched as Sheila slowly retrieved the photograph from her purse and with a deep breath showed it to Katie. There in the picture were Sheila, Wand and the two men in what seemed to be one of the local bars in New Orleans. Katie immediately recognized Clayton Jacobs from just a few days earlier. "He sat right here in this office last week," Katie said to herself, but loud enough that Sheila heard her. She shoved the picture back into her purse and turned to face Katie completely.

"He was here?" Sheila asked. Her face determined as she continued. "You interviewed Clay and Janice for the adoption of this baby?"

Katie just looked at Sheila. She couldn't decide rather the sound in her voice was shock and disbelief or determination. Before she could answer, Sheila began again.

"Katie, when did you do the interview? Did you meet Janice? She's really nice, huh?" Sheila asked.

"Wait. Slow down a minute." Katie stated. "I interviewed them last week and yes, I met Janice and she seemed to be a very nice person." Katie began to rub her temples with hopes of easing away the stress that was trying to settle behind her eyes. "Look, I have a few questions for you, Sheila," Katie said. "How did you meet them, because apparently, you know something of them as a couple."

Sheila tried to make herself comfortable again in the chair as she faced Katie. "There's this particular church Wanda and I would visit every now and again. The messages were inspiring but mostly we went to listen to the music being played on the pipe organ."

"I know just where you're talking about." Katie threw in. "But please continue."

"Well, one night they had a big something going on over there and anytime it's something big, they'll play the pipe organ. Anyway, we had just sat down, me and Wanda, and they had just started playing that song...... Holy, Holy, Holy...you know the one, right?" Sheila stopped waiting for Katie to say something. Katie was amazed at how Sheila was actually rambling out this extended version of her meeting the Jacobs.

"Sheila, I know the song. Now please get to the point." Katie replied.

"Yeah right. Sorry about that. Anyway, when the organist finished playing, she was introduced to the congregation as Mrs. Janice Jacobs. She used to live in New Orleans, her and Clay, years ago and they were members of the church. So, it was a kind of welcome home moment or something like that."

"How did you meet them, Sheila?" Katie sounded exhausted and a bit aggravated at the moment.

"I'm trying to tell you now if you'd let me finish," Sheila responded with a bit of a huff. "I didn't get formally introduced to them, but Wanda did. I was kinda standing off to the side admiring how good looking that man was."

Katie simply shook her head as she grinned slightly at Sheila's freshness. She wondered at that moment just how much different worlds she was from Sheila if she hadn't joined the convent. Sheila noticed the look on Katie's face and said, "What's wrong now?"

"Nothing. Just a thought came across my mind. Please continue." Katie encouraged.

"As I was saying", Sheila began again, "while we were leaving, I asked Wanda about them and she said that they were here for the convention. So, I was pretty much through with the whole matter, but a couple of nights later Wanda and I were at the bar and to be honest we were the one out there to fish!"

"So, this is the part when you finally got to meet and later get involved with a married man, right?" Katie put in at that moment with a very cynical look on her face.

Sheila could hear it in her voice and see it all over her face, which brought her up short. "Look, Katie, whatever you think you know about me and what happened with Clay I really suggest you hold up on your self-righteous judgment until you hear the end of the story or are you capable of doing that!?" Sheila was almost to the point of shouting. She was breathing rather briskly and she knew she had to calm herself down if she was going to finish this story.

"You're right. And I'm sorry I had no right to draw any conclusions about Clay and what he did to you." Katie said.

"Whoa wait," Sheila said with her hands held up in protest. "You really don't get it do you? Katie, Clayton Jacobs is more of a victim here then you can imagine. I was the seducer. I prayed upon his weakness. Listen. I wasn't looking for a relationship. I just wanted to have sex with the man and after pushing one drink after another on him, we brought him and his friend back to the house. We weren't ever together the whole night."

Katie couldn't believe all that she was hearing. She was seeing Sheila in a whole new light and she didn't like it. "So, you're telling me that all you and this man had was a quick romp in the sack and you got pregnant for your troubles?" Katie said.

Sheila studied the expression on Katie's face and then with a slight smile simply said, "That's basically the bottom line. Katie, I'm not telling you this to make you feel better and I don't even care if it changes your opinion of me. What I do care about is the status of this couple and exactly where were they on the list."

Katie reached for the folder that Sheila was now holding, but Sheila didn't let go. She looked at Katie with such concentration that she resigned to tell her, "They were number one choice to be the parents of your baby, but of course that all changes." Explained Katie.

"Why does it change, because of what I told you?" Sheila asked.

"Sheila," Katie countered, "you're keeping the baby remember? So, it doesn't matter."

But Sheila would not be deterred. "Then why hadn't you filed their folder away already and don't lie!" Sheila said.

"The reason is that I wrongfully thought that I needed to keep their folder close at hand if needed," Katie said. "As a matter of fact, you would not have known this much if you wouldn't have been looking on my desk." Now it was Katie's turn to feel offended. After all, it wasn't her fault that Sheila was in the mess she was in. "Look, Sheila, right now I don't know what to think. It's been a long day and we both could use a good night rest."

Sheila realized that Katie was trying to put an end to the conversation, but there were things she needed to know, things that only Sheila could tell. She took a calm breath and plunged in.

"Katie, I know you've had a rough day, and I haven't done anything to make it better, but I really need you to sit down and hear me out, please." Said Sheila.

Katie sat back down next to Sheila and with a sigh resigned to listen to the rest of the story. "Okay. I'll listen and I'll do my best to not past judgment."

"That's all I ask," Sheila responded. "Katie, the whole time I was with Clay all he talked about was his wife Janice and the troubles they'd faced over the years." Began Sheila. "You would think I was his counselor or something the way he talked to me. I begin to realize that Clayton Jacobs was not just a nice-looking older guy but a real decent family man. Katie, I assure you that if it weren't for the alcohol and my persistence, we never would have been together much less me being pregnant."

"So", Katie began, "you're telling me that Clay and you weren't an item but more of a one-night stand? What about Wanda and the other guy, were they involved too?"

"Not really." Sheila started. "I do think that they may have done it, but I can't be sure. You'd have to ask Wanda. I do know that for the rest of that night and especially the next day, I really got to see what a real man is."

"What do you mean?" Katie asked.

"Girl, what I'm about to tell you is gonna blow your mind, and I wouldn't have believed it myself if I weren't right there to see it with my own two eyes. The next day around noon, Clay called to say that he was about to leave town, but he wanted me to meet someone."

Katie realizing where this was going exclaimed, "Oh my Lord, Sheila, he didn't bring Janice over there did he?"

"Yes. That's exactly what he did, and believe you me, I was scared half to death. Anyway, Clay couldn't live with the fact that he had stepped out on Janice. So, he decided to come clean with her first thing that morning. They'd stayed at relatives while they were here and so it helped cushion the blow being around family members."

"So, then what happened?" Katie asked.

"Well, I can't lie. I hid in the hall closet the whole time they were up until I heard her ask Wanda to deliver a message to me. She remembered meeting Wanda and you could tell she felt that she was a part of the whole family which she was." Sheila was rambling again.

"Sheila, what was the message?" Katie persisted not believing how caught up she had become in this story. She knew that by the end of it she would have to decide about the "Jacobs."

"She said that she wanted to ask me a question that only I could answer." Said Sheila. "After a couple of minutes, I realized that I was acting like a child and that this woman did not come to fight, so I came out and made myself know and as soon as I saw her face to face, I felt so small." Sheila dropped her chin into her chest when she raised tears were sliding down her face. "She told me that she wasn't angry with me, but wanted to know what had she done to bring me to the point of wanting her husband. Katie, she even apologized as if she had offended me." Sheila explained. "I couldn't say nothing but no ma'am and yes ma'am to her questions. Then before she left, she asked me one more question and that was simply .... was it over? And I said Yes. Then she said that she would keep me in her prayers and then said goodbye."

Katie looked at Sheila in total disbelief. She was absolutely amazed at what she had just heard. Either Janice Jacobs was crazy or a real saint in ever since of the word.

"Sheila, I don't know what to say." Katie began. "I don't even know why are you saying all of this now. Has something changed?"

"Yes, Katie. I've changed my mind that is. I know, not think, but know that the best thing that I can give to my baby is a real fighting chance."

Katie felt like the room was spinning. She got up and went to her desk and opened her top drawer where she kept a container of aspirin. She opened them and poured two of them in her hand and popped them into her mouth. She took a swallow of the royal crown cola that had been sitting on her desk getting warm to wash the pills down. Then she looked at Sheila and slowly said, "So let me get this straight. You were at home and for whatever reason, you had a complete change of heart and decided to give the baby up for adoption which seems to be the best option for the child. Correct?"

"Correct," said Sheila.

"That's why you called and came down here to see me, right?" Katie asked.

"That's right," Sheila said.

Katie walked across the little office to stand in front of the window. The sun had crossed the skyline and was heading west. She looked down at the shadow that was being cast by the surrounding buildings. She turned back to face her friend. Her friend who had made a mistake was now paying a very high price. She went and sat back down beside Sheila and continued.

"So you come over here to tell me you've changed your mind, but while you're here you accidentally discover that the man that you had sex with and got pregnant for is one half of the couple that not only was interviewed by me but that I chose as the best fit for your baby, right?"

"That does sound crazy but that's right," Sheila said.

"One more question. So now that you know that Clayton and Janice Jacobs are qualified, would you want them to be this child's parents?" Katie asked.

Sheila smiled and said, "I wouldn't have it any other way. Katie, this is perfect!" Sheila said. "We couldn't have asked for a better outcome. My child being raised by his natural father and by a woman who will love him like it's her own. It doesn't get any better than that!"

"Oh right. Just hold on for a second. This is not a normal procedure we're talking about Sheila." Katie began to explain. Even though she'd known of families that had adopted children from less fortunate members of their family to keep the child within the family as a whole, but that was in California and it didn't involve the potential parents dealing with a child that so happens to be the product of an affair between the adoptive father and his former mistress. "Oh my gosh!" Katie exclaimed.

Sheila looked at the expression on Katie's face and wondered what had come across her mind. "What's wrong?" she asked.

"How do I explain this to the Reverend Mother?" Katie asked

"Oh, that's simple. You don't." Sheila said with a smile.

CHAPTER 12

For the next two days, everyone was in a whirl of activity. Sheila was doing her best to be as helpful as possible to Wanda around the house. She knew how her cousin had had to carry the load for both of them and it was really wearing her down. Katie hadn't come by since she and Sheila had that mind-boggling conversation, but she called on a couple of occasions to let Sheila know how things were going with getting everything back lined up. This morning the telephone rang and when Sheila answered, to her surprise it was the Reverend Mother. She'd called to speak with Sheila to make sure that she indeed was set on adoption and that she wouldn't change her mind again.

"No, ma'am." Sheila had said. "I assure you that I've definitely made up my mind and this is what's best for my child."

"Certainly, my dear, and we share your concerns as to what's best for the child which brings me to my next point," said Reverend Mother. "Sister Wells has informed me that you have been highly adamant in the selection of the potential parents. Is that correct, my dear?" asked the Reverend Mother.

The truth being told she was quite taken aback by what she called an illogical act of the youth. She'd instructed Katie to contact the James family even though Katie had explained that Sheila specifically requested that her baby be given to the Jacobs family. When Katie spoke to them, they weren't at all receptive to the idea and informed Katie that they would have to think about it and that they would call back if they were still interested. This turn of events really put the Reverend Mother in a disagreeable mood. She'd insisted on talking to Sheila herself to see whether the child, as she put it, was indeed thinking of her own accord or was she being in some way influenced by others. Katie knew all too well that the Reverend Mother was referring to her. She hadn't liked the idea of Katie being such close friends with Sheila and Wanda. She'd often wondered what was so interesting about those two women that would keep Sis Wells so captivated. She'd conclude that whatever the influence was it was unhealthy for the still young and naïve Katie. She'd began dropping little hints as of late about Katie spending more time at the abbey with some of the other sisters, and less time in the areas (as she would put it) of the less fortunate. This all fell on deaf ears as Sis Katie was concerned. Now she was trying to dissuade Sheila in her choice of the Jacobs family.

"That is correct Mother and I'm sure that sis Wells informed you of my choice?" Sheila asked in a not so sweet manner. She didn't too much care for the Reverend Mother. She came over as being snobbish, and she didn't like the way she treated Katie either. She'd prepared herself for this contest of wills. She by no means would be backed down or pushed around by this woman. As far as she was concerned, there was too much at stake.

"Sis Wells has indeed spoken to me about your choice. Exactly why do you think the Jacobs family would be what's best for this child?" said the Reverend Mother.

"Firstly ma'am, this child is still my child until I decide to give, he or she up. Secondly, I am familiar with this family from sharing the same religious background." Sheila said even though she knew she was stretching pretty think following this path.

"So, you are a member of their church?" Mother said. She already knew that the Jacobs weren't in any congregations in the New Orleans area.

"Actually, no I'm not. The Methodist church that I attend was once the home church of the Jacobs family and they visit it from time to time." Sheila responded.

"I see. So, I take it that you have some idea about their financial status as well?" said the Reverend Mother.

This was low Sheila believed, but it fit in regards to the type of person she thought the Reverend Mother was. "No. I don't know the specifics of their financial status. I do, however, know that they were considered as one of the top applicants for this adoption." Sheila paused for just a second for the last statement to sink in, then she went on to the offensive. "Tell me something, Mother," she began, "isn't it true that you are already well aware of each couple's financial status and the interviews are offered to those who have already met that standard, correct?"

"Yes child, this is correct, but I don't...." Reverend Mother began, but Sheila was on a roll.

"Isn't it also correct that one of your personal references is that the couples be of the Catholic faith?" Sheila asked. This was her ace in the hole, and she hoped she hadn't played it too soon. There was a very long pause and Sheila took this as a signal to press on for the final blow. "Hello Mother, are you still there?" Sheila asked knowing full well that the Reverend was still on the line.

"Ah, yes my dear. I'm still here, but I'm not quite sure what you're getting at." Reverend Mother finally responded.

"What I'm driving at is that I'm not Catholic and neither is the Jacobs family. The James family, your preferred couple, however, are Catholic." Sheila paused for a split second then continued. "You also aren't too thrilled with the fact that Sis Wells has befriended me and my cousin as she has. Is that also because we're not Catholic as well?"

"Young lady, I can assure you that this is certainly not the case. It may seem a bit odd when you look at it from a certain point of view, but you must understand that I want only what's best for your child." Said Reverend.

"Well, I'm so glad to hear that because I am definitely set on the idea of having what's best for my child. Therefore, I'd gladly see her or she raised Methodist!"

"My dear, uh Sheila, correct?" Reverend Mother began.

"That's correct, Mother," Sheila responded.

"Let me assure you that we do not wish to bring injury to you in any manner. We intend to see that this child get the best available care and parenting there is to offer." Mother said. "There is a matter of age that should be considered as well. You see we feel that a couple that is as well along in years as the Jacobs would not be a sound choice for the welfare and future of the child," said Mother. She hoped that this last argument, though transparent as it was, would stall the tide of this very persistent young woman. She was wrong.

"Mother, I don't know what you're trying to pull, but I know for a fact that the Jacobs are both in good sound health, and have been a part of this state's foster care program for several years. Are you now trying to say they are unfit physical as well as spiritually too?" Sheila asked.

"Oh, gracious not, not at all!" said Mother. "I only meant that it is a possibility that they couldn't handle a newborn on through adulthood. We certainly wouldn't want that to happen to the child."

"What I wouldn't want is to have my child placed in a home-based upon its religious connections only to be raised by a couple who have no experience with children and are so caught up in their careers that they don't even know if they want to adopt anyway." Sheila almost shouted through the phone. She'd realized that she'd made a grave mistake by letting on that she knew that the James had not returned the calls from the office of the Reverend Mother. Her assistant, who was really fond of Katie, yet terrified of Mother Reverend, shared this information with Katie under the strictest of confidence. Well, she was sorry for breaking both of their trust. She'd deal with them later; this was way too important not to utilize.

"How did you find this out young lady?" said Reverend in a tone that could have split ice.

"That information is for me to know and expose as I see fit, Mother!" snapped Sheila. She was no longer trying to even feign politeness.

"Young lady, how dare you take that tone with me!" exclaimed Reverend Mother.

"I will continue to take this tone with you and anyone else that tries to force me into giving my baby up to a program that is prejudiced in its selections!" Sheila shot back. "Maybe I need to get in contact with the New Orleans NAACP and C.O.R.E. offices in order to shed some light on the way you're running things over here at the hospital. By the time the newspapers get finished with you, you'll be shipped to a monastery so far from here till you can't find your way back!"

After a very long silence, Reverend Mother answered, "Very well then. Since there's no changing your mind, we'll go with our first choice the Jacobs family. Take good care of yourself."

"You too goodbye." Said, Sheila and hung up. "The nerve of some people," Sheila said to herself as she walked to the kitchen. Just then, Wanda walked through the door looking all flustered.

"Hey girl, what's happening?" Sheila said over her shoulder. She looked at the clock on the wall and realized that Wanda was probably kept over at the plant. Sheila bent over to get the old beat up washbasin that she and Wanda sometimes used to soak their feet in. She sat it on the counter then took the carton of Epson salt out of the cabinet and poured some in the basin. Then she took the tea kettle and filled it up with water and placed it on the stove to heat.

"Wanda", Sheila called, "don't go to sleep on the sofa. I'm fixing some eggs and bacon for you. Now come in here, because I can't drag you anymore!" After a couple of minutes, Wanda staggered her way into the kitchen. She sat in the chair closest to her and placed her head on the table. "Rough night huh?" Sheila asked as she walked behind the chair Wanda was sitting in.

Wanda moaned as Sheila rubbed the back of her neck. "Girl if I didn't know any better, I'd swear them white folks down at the plant are personally trying to work me like a sugar mill jackass," Wanda said as she sat up from the table.

This comment brought a laugh to Sheila's heart. She reached down and hugged Wanda's neck and said, "Well, at least you're off for the next couple of days. Here, put your feet in this basin and I'll pour the water over them." Sheila said.

The kettle wasn't hot enough to start whistling, but it was warm enough to soak one's feet in. As she gently poured the water into the basin, Wanda let out a long sigh of relief. "Lordy ham mercy! Chile that sho' nuff feels good!" Wanda said.

Sheila went to the sink and refilled the kettle and put it back on the stove. Then she checked the strips of bacon that were frying in the skillet. They were almost ready. "How do you want your eggs cuz?" Sheila asked Wanda over her shoulder while getting the eggs out of the icebox.

"You feel like cooking this morning, huh?" Wanda said as she moved her feet around leisurely in the warm water.

"I don't mind at all. It's the least I can do with you having to do all the hard work." Sheila said. She was about to start telling Wanda how much she appreciated her and how she owed her, but before she could get started this time around, Wanda waved her off.

"Sheila, don't start that mess this morning. We've known each other all our lives." Wanda said. Hell, we more like sisters than cousins and I know that if the shoe was on the other foot you would do the same for me, or at least I hope." Wanda said.

"Of course, I would. Now, what about these eggs, woman?" Sheila said with a smile.

"Sunnyside up would be perfect. Thanks, sis." Wanda said with a wink at Sheila when she faced her.

"For you sis," Sheila began, "anything at all."

"So, did you sleep last night?" Wanda asked Sheila as she watched her pour a cup of coffee.

Sheila brought the steaming liquid over to Wanda and sat it in front of her. Then Sheila answered, "You mean did I have that same crazy dream again last night." Sheila said.

"Well, did you?" Wanda persisted.

"Yeah," Sheila began as she fixed a plate of food for Wanda. "It's just so strange. I keep getting on the bus and when I sit down, I'm pregnant, but after we ride for about a block or two my stomach disappears."

Wanda spoke between mouthfuls. "I think that your dreams mean something Sheila," Wanda said as she chewed a piece of bacon. She took a sip of coffee and continued. "Did the dream end like the other ones?" she asked.

Sheila sat down with her own plate and a glass of orange juice. "That's the part that's really getting on my nerves. I get to our street and I get up to get off the bus, but then I wake up with this feeling that something is missing." Sheila explained. She took a swallow of juice and continued. "It's as if I know that I'm no longer pregnant and my life is supposed to be going along just fine, but then when it's time to get off the bus it's like I'm missing something or losing something."

Wanda looked at Sheila and placed her hand on top of Sheila's hand when she finished talking. "Look, Sheila," Wanda began, "I'm not some head doctor or one of the women on Bourbon street that can read your palms or tell you what your dreams mean, but I do believe God is trying to show you something and one day He will," Wanda said as she at the last of her eggs and drank the remainder of her coffee.

"I just don't want anything to go wrong right now," Sheila said. "It was enough I had to set the so-called Reverend Mother straight about my baby and who he or she will go to."

Wanda was drying her feet off with the towel Sheila had placed on the back of the chair. She had been informed by Sheila about the Jacobs applying for the right to adopt the baby. Once Wanda had learned this, she was even more adamant about this being part of the plan of God. She'd told Sheila the same night that she came back from the hospital that any dang fool could see that God has a special plan for this baby and that we had to do everything possible to make sure nothing got in the way.

"Girl, I'm telling you," Wanda had said that night, "God is up to something! Think about it, Sheila. What are the chances that out of all the couples who put in to adopt this here baby the one couple that stands out is the one who is the father of the child?" After she'd finished with her feet, she got up and quickly went to her bedroom to change out of her work clothes. Sheila cleaned the table and smiled as she noticed that neither she nor her cousin had left anything on their plates. She sat the dirty dishes in the sink and ran hot water in order to wash them. Wanda came in at that moment.

"So, what did that heifer have to say?" Wanda began as she went to the stove with her cup in hand to pour herself another cup of coffee.

"Wanda, if you drink another cup you know you won't be able to go back to sleep anytime soon," Sheila said as she washed one of the plates they just used.

"I'll get some sleep later. Remember I'm off for the next two days. Now back to my question," Wanda persisted. She really had no love or even a little like for the Reverend Mother. She felt that Katie should handle the whole adoption business which would be best for everyone concerned.

"Can you believe the woman had the nerve to call here this morning and try to pressure me into changing my mind about giving my baby to Clay and Janice!?" Sheila exclaimed.

"What did you tell her?" Wanda asked as she took a sip of her coffee while she sat back down.

"Hell No! Well, not in those words, but she definitely has no more doubts that the only people I want my baby adopted by is the Jacobs family." She said as she sat down.

"Do you want me to call that hospital and let that woman have a piece of my mind?" Wanda said already halfway out of the chair.

"Girl, No. Sit back down." Sheila said as she grabbed Wanda by the hand. "Believe me when I tell you that when I finished with that woman, she was more than glad to get off the telephone with me."

"Good for you honey," Wanda said. "Have you talked to Katie yet?"

"Oh, I think I'll be hearing from her real soon. Especially after what I said to her precious Reverend Mother," Sheila began. "I just hope she doesn't get into too much trouble."

Wanda looked at Sheila for a long second then said, "Sheila, what did you say that would get Katie in trouble."

"Well, I was so mad at the time that I let it slip that I knew about the other couple who had been also interested in adopting," Sheila said with a voice so low it was almost a whisper.

"Sheila!" Wanda exclaimed, "You know you weren't supposed to mention that! You could get Katie fired!"

"That won't happen," Sheila said with a smug look on her face.

"How come you so confident that it won't happen?" Wanda pressed.

"Because I told the mighty Reverend Mother that if she as so much tries to interfere with this adoption in any way whatsoever I would go straight to the NAACP and CORE offices and report how she is selecting applications based upon their religious affiliations," Sheila finished with breath to spare. "It's like racial profiling. You know how people are picked for the better jobs simply because they are white and mainly because we're not," Sheila said.

Wanda crossed her arms and began to digest all this information that she'd just heard. She even began to wonder what would happen if she went to the Bishop at the Methodist church to inform them of what was being done. This could even be a help to Katie if handled right.

"I'll tell you one thing, cuz. Reverend Mother doesn't realize what she's up against," said Wanda. "I'm going to go take a little nap but you call Katie and tell her to get over here this afternoon."

CHAPTER 13

Katie began to climb the steps to Wanda and Sheila's house. It had been a hot day and the afternoon didn't show any signs of cooling off. She knocked on the door and looked out across the street at some of the children that were outside playing. "Playing in all that heat," Katie thought to herself. "Just enough to get a heatstroke!" She turned to know again when the door begins to open and Wanda appeared at the door.

"Hey girl, come on in," was all Wanda said as she turned and walked back into the house. "I got some ice-cold lemon sweet tea just the way you like it!" Wanda said as she went to the kitchen. "Come on in here girl and grad a seat and cool off." Wanda urged her friend.

"I don't know if it would be wise for me to be around sharp objects. By the way, where's Sheila?" Katie said with more than a hint of irritation in her voice.

"She's in her room waiting to see if it's safe," Wanda said with a grin.

"I don't know how safe it's gonna be, but ain't no use her hidin'. Sheila!" Wanda yelled. "Come on out and take your medicine." Wanda poured Katie a big glass of tea and then poured one for herself.

"You sure Katie ain't gonna kill me?" Sheila yelled back from the bedroom.

"Girl, bring yo' ass out here! You owe me one mighty big apology!" Yelled Katie. She looked over at Wanda, who's mouth was still open at what she'd just heard. "What?" Katie asked indignantly.

"Uh, I just didn't think you use that kind of language before." Wanda finally said.

"That's because I haven't been this angry at someone in a very long time." Katie snapped.

At that moment the bedroom door cracked open just enough that Sheila stuck her arm through waving a white bra hoping to enter in peace. "Is it safe to come out now?" Sheila said from behind the door.

Wanda and Katie were already laughing at Sheila's waving her bra as a white flag, to begin with. "Girl, come out here," Katie said through bits of laughter. "Besides, I would never hit a woman with a child. Now after the child is born that's a different story," said Katie.

Wanda got up and went to yank Sheila out the bedroom door. "Girl, bring yo' butt, on out here! We ain't got time for all this foolishness." Wanda said.

Sheila followed Wanda out with little resistance to her pull. She pulled the chair out as she looked at Katie. She eased into the chair and smiled at Katie as she mouthed the words, "I'm sorry."

Katie crossed her arms over her chest and spoke, "What's that? I can't hear you. Did you hear anything Wanda?" Katie asked.

"Nope, not a word," responded Wanda.

Sheila knew they weren't going to make this easy for her. Sheila cleared her throat and said, "Katie, I really am sorry for letting Reverend Mother know that I knew about the James family, but if you would just give me a chance, I can explain the whole thing," Sheila continued. She gave a sidelong look at Wanda for support.

"Don't look at me. You on your own" was all Wanda would say and as a show of support for Katie's position, she crossed her arms over her chest too.

"Well first of all," Sheila began again, "I didn't want to tell her at all."

"Then why did you?" demanded Katie.

This was not starting off at all as she had hoped. "As I was about to say. I didn't even have her on my mind. She called me and started trying to convince me to change my mind about the Jacobs to adopt my baby." She explained. "She kept pressing the issue and all until I had gotten pretty heated." Katie took a deep breath as she closed her eyes. Both Sheila and Wanda knew that this was a sign that their friend was very upset and trying to calm herself down. "Katie," Sheila said, "I know now that I probably could have and should have at least tried to handle the situation differently, but you've got to understand that at that moment I felt I had to do what was best."

Wanda sat watching both women deal with their emotions. Both were under so much pressure. Sheila at the very end of her term having to deal with out of control hormones and emotions and Katie completely stressed out due to pressures on the job, being excepted by the powers that be, and still not quite sure if being a nun was what she really wanted anyway. Wanda silently realized that this incident could likely bring an end to the relationship between the two. She wanted to say something, anything, to try to ease the tension that had built up so quickly. She still remained silent.

"Sheila, listen to me carefully," Katie began. "From the day we met on the bus that morning, I believe that it was God's will that we meet." Katie slowly uncrossed her arms and placed her hands on the table. She started to twist the small ring on her right pinky as she continued to speak. "Since then we've become good friends, all three of us. Yes, I'm not always happy at the abbey and I won't lie, I don't like the Reverend Mother, probably less than you both do," said Katie as she got up from the chair and walked over to the window. "There were times when I felt so alone out here." Katie began again. You could hear the tremble in her voice as she continued. "Y'know I was about to pack my things and go back to California, but then I met you, Sheila." She turned to face the two women with tears now trailing down her cheeks. "It was as if God had given me now one but two sisters." The room was thick with emotions and now all three were crying.

"Katie," Wanda slowly began, "I want you to know that I need you and that you are special to us both. When I came to New Orleans, I was running from a past that I wanted so dearly to forget, but that could never happen as long as I had my son. I love him, but I can't be all that he needs me to be. That's why he's still back in Mississippi." Wanda at that moment got up and went over to Katie. She took both of Katie's hands into hers and slowly said, "I know how you feel when it comes to loneliness. There were times I was just about ready to die.

I couldn't sleep because when I'd fall asleep, I dream about my baby. I'd wake up sweating and on top of that, the dreams made me feel so guilty that I couldn't eat. I had lost a lot of weight and I was living like I was a robot, but I prayed until something happened and that something was Sheila."

Wanda put her arm around Katie's shoulders and with her other hand reached for Sheila. Sheila got up and walked over to take Wanda's outstretched arm. All the while she stared through the tear-filled eyes at Katie. The one she'd betrayed. Her mind flashed back to when she was a child at church listening to old Reverend Jones preach about the last supper and how Peter had told the Lord that he'd go with him to the very end. Yet he denied that he even knew him. He'd betrayed the Lord and she'd betrayed her friend. The friend who had stuck to her and cared for her better than any sister could. All this in such a short period of time. It had only been a few weeks, yet it felt as if she'd known Katie forever. She had to make this right somehow. She thought about Peter again, and how he wept and repented of his actions. She could do it too. She had to, but could Katie forgive her as Jesus did? She reached out to touch Katie's hand and when she didn't flinch away, she gently took hold of it and softly began to speak.

"Katie, I was wrong in betraying your trust. I was selfish and self-centered and I can't use the excuse that I'd do anything to protect my child because what I did was wrong." She took a deep breath to still herself and continued. "I can't change what I did but I can say that I do not want to lose you like my other big sister. If you can find it in your heart to forgive me, I promise I'll never do or say anything again that would put this friendship in harm's way."

"We both love you, Katie," Wanda whispered, "and we always want you to be a part of our lives. No matter what you decide to do, we love you." Katie looked deeply into the eyes of Wanda and knew that her words were true. She knew in Wanda she had a sister who would be an anchor, a confidant, and a counselor. Sheila who was the shortest of the three women looked up at Katie with an air of expectation. Katie knew that in those eyes was a fire that would burn red hot when she or whatever she loved was threatened. She believed that Sheila considered her no longer as just a friend but someone she loved. What Sheila did was in truth something that would demand some form of disciplinary action against Katie. This she well knew, yet something deep inside of her very being continued to ask the question: If I were in her shoes, would I have done no less for the well-being of my child? Now with Sheila standing in front of her, she glanced down at her stomach and then at her own flat belly. In that instance, she knew without a shadow of a doubt that if it were her, she would have done the same thing. "No," Katie whispered. It was settled in that moment of decision. She would forgive Sheila and move on. This was a lesson in life that she was being taught and she would remember it always.

"God forgives and we should just as much forgive others even as He forgives us." Katie thought. She smiled at Sheila and simply said, "If I lose my job, you better help me find another one." They all burst into a fit of laughter and hugged one another.

It was as if someone let the air out the ball the way the tension in the room faded away. Sheila just couldn't seem to stop talking. She went on and on to Katie about how she and Reverend Mother debated about the baby's interest.

"So, then I told her," Sheila was saying while Katie sipped on her second glass of tea, "that I would indeed contact the NAACP and the CORE offices to tell them exactly what she was doing in the adoption placement program."

"And that's when she had a change of heart, right?" This was Wanda speaking. She wasn't really level headed about these things and she really felt that a little more pressure should be brought against the Reverend Mother to make sure she not only held true to leaving the adoption process alone but leave Katie alone too. "Ladies, I really think we need to go visit Bishop," said Wanda. Katie sat up to object, but before she could say anything, Wanda quieted her. "Listen. We need to make sure that not only will Sheila's adoption goes as planned but see to it that you're safe too." Wanda said.

"Gosh," Katie sighed into her hands. "You make it sound as if Reverend Mother's dead set on getting me! Reminds me of those old gangster movies we'd watch at the movies back in California." She shook her head slightly then said, "Look, I do realize and appreciate all that you think is necessary to do to protect me, but I honestly don't want to slander her name no matter my personal feelings towards her."

Sheila wanted to say something but thought better of it. She didn't want anything to happen to Katie and as far as she was concerned, whatever happened to the Reverend Mother was her own fault. Yet, she realized that this would deeply affect Katie in other ways. She knew how serious Katie was about her religious convictions. Katie believed what she read in that bible she carried around. She'd believed so much that she left everything she knew to come to New Orleans to follow as she put it "the call of God." Sheila remembered how Katie had explained that the changes she'd gone through were of no consequence when compared to the grace of God working in her life. "I've been through so many changes" she had said to her and Wanda, and that "most of the time when things are supposed to be normal, I don't know how to respond." She'd seen a lot of people hurt in the demonstrations brought about by the movement and she truly believed that the very core of the movement was God's way of bringing people into the light and showing them that He loved all of His creation. His love was equal and not discriminative. God's love was freely given to all people. God, in her opinion, gave everything for people of every nation, color or gender with no exceptions made for social class. She further believed that people were supposed to love other people the same way, thus showing the love of God working through them. She sincerely believed that God didn't want people suffering from needless hunger, sickness or disease.

"There is entirely too much money in this country for people to be homeless and barely surviving." Katie had told Sheila just a couple of days earlier.

"We can't depend on the government to make things right," Sheila had responded to Katie's comment.

"Exactly and that's why we have to be the difference makers. I believe I'm a difference-maker and everything that I've faced has been a part of the lesson plan of God. Sheila snapped back to the present moment as Wanda was telling Katie that a little extra insurance for their sakes wouldn't hurt.

"I'm not saying that we have to actually get the Bishop and our church involved, but it would be good for them to at least know what's going on," Wanda said.

"I think," Sheila began, "that whatever we do Wanda, we can't directly involve Katie it at all possible." She looked at Katie just as Katie was trying to figure out where Sheila was going with this. Sheila reached across the table and patted Katie on the back of her hand, then said to Wanda, "Wanda, even though I think we should not only go see the Bishop, but be prepared to talk to both movement agencies, but I'm willing to hold back until it's necessary. We can't put our sister in spiritual harm's way by trying to protect her from a physical threat."

Wanda looked at Sheila then over to Katie. She could see the tension in her face and wonder if it was from worrying about Sheila and the baby and what the Reverend Mother would do, or was it something more. Something she had missed.

"Katie, do you feel that way?" Wanda asked.

Katie took a deep breath and said, "I believe that God will fight this battle if I'm obedient to let Him. This what we're going through is only gonna make us stronger and wiser. We just have to learn to trust God and watch him work it all out." Katie said.

"What if it doesn't turn out for the best for all of us?" Wanda asked. Sheila waited to hear the response that Katie would give because she too had the same question lingering in the back of her mind.

"Not my will, but let His will be done. And in His will, we will all have what's best for us all." Katie said.

"So, I guess that this is one of those lessons of life or whatever you call it kinda things, huh?" Wanda asked.

"It's lessons learned in life Wanda," Sheila corrected. "I just don't know which one this one is supposed to be." She concluded.

"Simple," Katie said smiling as she got up to leave, "it's the lesson of trust. So, let's just trust God for the best and I'll see you both, tomorrow." And with that, Katie left out of the house.

CHAPTER 14

"Yes uh, thank you and uh what time do we need to be down there for?" asked Janice. She was shaking so much she could barely hold the receiver.

Katie sat at her desk with a huge smile on her face as she spoke to Janice Jacobs. She could picture the expression on the woman's face. She had just told her that she and her husband Clayton were selected to be the adoptive parents for Sheila's baby. The baby who accidentally had been fathered by Clay Jacobs on an excursion he and one of his running buddies had while in New Orleans attending of all things, a church conference with their wives. Just thinking about it made Katie dizzy.

"Mrs. Jacobs, as I said earlier, you and your husband won't have to come up here until the baby is born," Katie explained.

"Well, will you or can you give me some idea as to how soon it may be?" Janice asked. She was already prepared to take a leave of absence from work. The question was when.

"There aren't any problems are there Mrs. Jacobs?" Katie asked. This would be absolutely terrible if for some reason or another the Jacobs couldn't take the child. "No, stop it, Katie," she said to herself. "Just trust God. He's working it all out for everyone's good." She reminded herself.

"Oh no, there's no problem. I just wanted to have an idea of how quickly this all could happen. My husband would need to take off from his job and it would be easier for him to do so with a couple of day's notice." Janice explained. She really wanted to go to New

Orleans right now and wait for the baby to be born, but she really wanted Clay to be with her and their new baby.

"Finally, after all these years and all those tears I've cried, God answered my prayers," Janice said half to herself and Katie.

"Well, I'm so glad that He has done just that," Katie responded. "It's about trusting Him," Janice said. "Well, Mrs. Jacobs, I wish I could talk a while longer, but I've got a lot of work to do so if you will excuse me, I have to go," Katie said. She really enjoyed talking to Janice. She was so refreshing.

"Okay. Well, I'll be waiting to hear from you. Thank you again, and God bless you," Janice said.

"God bless you too, goodbye," Katie said and hung up. She thought about how good of a mother Janice would be. She smiled to herself and began to finish up the last bit of paperwork necessary when Reverend Mother walked in. Katie knew it was her by the smell of the hospital's cleaning supplies and flowers. She was a walking combination of Lysol and glade air freshener. She grinned to herself as she wondered what the market worth of such a fragrance would be.

"My, my, don't we look happy this morning," said Mother, "I hope that some of this happiness will spill over into your hapless work performance."

So, this was her angle this morning, attack her by making allegations about her ability to do her job. "Well, she can try all she likes. I will not crumble under her pressure," Katie thought.

"Good morning, Mother. What can I do for you?" Katie said as polite as she thought possible even though her words had a certain bite to them.

"Well, I came down to see how the arrangements, for the Jacob's adoption, was coming. We wouldn't want any last-minute problems, now would we?" Mother said.

Katie did not like the sound of that, so as she went back to her paperwork she casually asked, "Do you anticipate any problems, Mother?" She would play her little game just long enough to figure out what her angle was.

"Oh, I was just thinking about some of the situations I've run into over the years. Mothers changing their minds, problems with documentation, falsifying documents, things like that. By the way, who is the father of the child?" she asked.

"So, this is what you're planning," Katie said to herself as she tried to hurriedly gather her thoughts.

"That's a very good question, Mother. Have you had an opportunity to ask Sheila about the father?" Katie responded in as nonchalant of way possible. She couldn't let on anything, not now at least. There was still too much at stake.

"I noticed," continued Mother, "that on her personal contact records, she's listed as being from Mississippi but she left the blank open where the question of fathering the child is asked." She paused just for the slightest moment as she fingered her rosary then continued. "You wouldn't by any chance know why the blank was left unanswered do you," said Mother. "Actually, I didn't take the original application on Sheila. I picked it up from the outpatient clinic." Katie said.

"Yes, of course, well you can certainly fill it in for her. I'm quite sure that she's told you who the father is since you're both so close," said Mother.

"Actually, Mother, she's told me about a situation regarding a certain main, but still I have my doubts," Katie said. She knew this response would cause Mother to either expose what she knew or show that she was grasping at straws.

"After all, she has admitted that she has been to bed with more than one man," Katie said as she leaned towards Mother, as what she said was confidential.

"I see," said Mother. "Well, surely she has some idea who the real father is of course," Mother continued.

"Well, to be totally frank with you, Mother, and this is the saddest part," Katie said as she brought her voice down to a whisper. She paused and walked to the door to close it and whispered to Mother, "Sheila has not only practiced fornication but openly enticed married men into committing adultery!" Katie said.

Mother gasped and made the sign of the cross. "The shame of it all," she said to Katie.

"Well, this is one of the many unfortunate cases where the young have gone astray and fallen under the bondage of Satan. I truly hope that with all that time you're spending with her that you've been counseling her to amend her ways." Reverend Mother expressed.

She wanted to have climbed up her sanctimonious high horse which in most cases was rather a bit discouraging, to say the least, but in this case, Katie encouraged her to follow her path of self-proclaimed righteousness to get Mother off the track where Sheila's baby's father was.

"Well if the child's father was indeed a product of adulterous behavior, we may be wise to leave such information out of the records." Mother concluded.

"Well, I must agree with you on this, Mother," Katie said trying to sound as much as a good pupil of the Reverend Mother as possible.

"Funny that you would since you don't seem to agree on anything else, I say, but we'll remedy that later on," she said and walked out the office.

Katie shut the door behind Mother as she walked out into the outer office area. She found herself leaning against the now-closed door for support. "Whew", said Katie exhaling loudly. She felt as if she'd been holding her breath the whole time Mother was there. Now she was gasping for air as if she were hyperventilating. She went to the small table behind her desk where she kept a picture of water and glasses. She poured herself a glass of water and drank it down in one sitting. She felt parched. She truly hadn't expected to have the Reverend Mother inquire about the father of Sheila's baby. What if she had some idea of who the real father was? "No, it's not possible," Katie knew that Clayton Jacobs was about to officially become the adoptive father to his natural son or daughter. One thing for sure, and that was that Mother was searching. Katie knew why, but she had to find out who was helping her. There could only be one person who would or could notice or identify any odd or peculiar points of interest. Katie looked at the clock on the wall. It was three o'clock in the afternoon. She dialed the number to Sheila and Wanda's house.

"Hello," said Wanda.

"It's me, Wanda. I need you to whip up a good ole fashion home-cooked meal," Katie said.

"Girl, hot as it is today, are you crazy?" exclaimed Wanda who for once had gotten off work at a normal time.

"Look, I know this sounds strange, but we may be able to prevent a major problem if we move quickly. It has to do with Clayton and Sheila," Katie said as she began to lock the file cabinets and tidy up her desk.

"What's going on?" Wanda asked

"I don't have time to explain but make sure Sheila is there, too. I'll be bringing a guest with me so be ready to follow my lead in whatever I say, okay? Wanda, I really need you to trust me on this." Katie said.

"Okay," Wanda finally said. "I'll see you soon," and they both hung up.

CHAPTER 15

Janice sat there for over fifteen minutes slowly crying to herself, but this time they weren't tears due to disappointments, delays or denials. This time she had won. This time God had heard her cries and blessed her. These were tears of complete joy. Janice was over now the shock of all that Katie Wells had told her on the phone. It all was finally sinking in. Janice got up from the table and went to her bedroom. She walked over to her dresser and looked at her reflection in the mirror. She was smiling and her smile turned to giggles that flowed from her heart. She would be a mother. God had finally moved for her and her husband. It was a miracle that in her mind was well overdue.

"Oh my God, I've got so much to do and get ready for," she exclaimed.

She opened her closet and took out the safety lockbox they kept on the top shelf behind her church hats. She set it on the bed and turned to get the key that she kept on a string at the bottom of the chest of drawers. She bent down and removed the bottom drawer, and there on the string was the key hanging in place by a tack. She removed it and went to the bed and opened the box. She and Clay kept a lot of their most important documents in this box – house deed, life insurance policies, both their birth certificates and a brown envelope with $750 they'd been saving just for this day. She took the money out and hurriedly counted and recounted it. Then she took half of the money and placed the rest back into its place. She closed the drawer just in time to hear a knock at the door. She hurried out to the living room and the door. It was Clay with both his arms loaded with groceries he'd gone to the store for. Janice opened the door with such vigor that she surprised clay.

"Hey, baby!" he said. "Thanks for opening the door. I wasn't sure you could hear me knocking." Janice reached to take two of the bags and went to the kitchen smiling so big that it caused Clay to ask, "My, my, don't you look really happy today. What's going on babe?"

Janice didn't answer but started to put up the items that were purchased. Clay watched her whirl around the kitchen with a zeal that he hadn't seen in years.

"Okay girl, what's going on with you?" Clayton asked his wife as she put up the last of the items.

Clay walked up to her from behind and fondled her on the shoulder and to his immediate surprise and joy, Janice spun around wrapping her arms around Clay's neck and kissed him with such passion that he was instantly aroused. The kiss was long and passionate and at this point in their marriage was uncommon and quite rare.

As she slowly separated from her husband but lingered in his arms, she whispered, "Y'know, you still know how to light my fire."

Clayton Jacobs was absolutely stunned by these changes of events, and later in years to come, he would remember that day and the ones that followed as the most exciting moments of his life with Janice.

"Janice, what you and that woman next door been smoking?" clay said in a joking manner. Such comments he knew would not normally set well with his sensible level headed wife, but this was turning more and more to be a day of abnormalities.

"The only thing that I'm high on is you, Mr. Clayton Jacobs." Janice seductively purred to her husband. She untangled herself from their embrace and began to pull him to their bedroom. Janice pushed her husband down on the bed and for the next forty-five minutes, Mr. and Mrs. Clayton Jacobs were newlyweds all over again.

Clay sat on the edge of the bed looking at the clock on the nightstand. It was now six o'clock in the morning and the sun was rising fast. It was Saturday morning and his usual routine was already laid out for him. First, get up, spend his normal 10 minutes in the bathroom, finish dressing, go to the kitchen and put on a pot of coffee. Even though he loved Janice's cooking, he tended to prefer to fix his own breakfast. It helped him order his thoughts and his morning he had a lot to order in his mind. He pulled out a slab of bacon and began to cut slices to fry. He liked his bacon on the thick side, so he didn't bother to have it sliced at the meat counter in the market that they shopped at. He took three eggs out of the refrigerator and set them on the empty plate he was using. Then he proceeded to light the burner on the stove. He took the biggest skillet in the kitchen and sat it over the fire. Then he placed the bacon into fry. It would make its own grease and after about five minutes he turned it over for the second time. It was nice and brown, and the aroma was intoxicating. He put on the baker's mitt and took the skittle off the fire and poured the excess grease into the old lard jar and placed the skillet back on the fire. With his fork, he pushed the bacon far enough over into the skillet to make room for his eggs. Then he lowered the flame and expertly cracked each egg into the skillet. He broke the yokes because he liked his eggs soft fried but thoroughly cooked. After everything was done, he took his plate of bacon and eggs along with a couple of slices of toast and sat down to dig in. After eating, he knew he had to mow the lawn, trim the hedges and after that, he would go and hand out with the fellows at the barbershop. Maybe even go help Daddy B with his cars. This is how a normal day was spent, but after last night, his normal was about to change.

    He poured himself another cup of coffee and often quickly washing the few dishes he had dirtied; he went to look in on Janice. He opened the door to their bedroom just enough to stick his head in. She was still fast asleep. This wasn't like her to be asleep at a little past seven o'clock, but then again, neither was her actions of last night. He eased the door shut and walked out into the hall out the front door and sat down on the front porch. By the looks of things, he could tell that it was gonna be a hot one today. Still, at this time of the morning, it was really nice. The birds were singing and the neighbors were just starting to stir.

    "Who was that woman?" he said to himself.

    It had been ages since they'd acted so passionately towards each other. It was as if twenty years had rolled back and Janice was as energetic and downright amazing as she'd ever been. Yet, he still was baffled as to why. Clayton sipped on his coffee and was about to light up a cigarette when he heard the screen door behind him open and close. Janice cane and eased down next to her husband.

"Good morning, honey," She said as she gave Clay a soft kiss on the cheek.

"Good morning to you, sleepyhead!" Clay answered. "You usually are up and in that flower garden by now pruning rose bushes."

Janice yawned and slipped her arm around Clay's and said as she looked out over the yard, "We usually go straight to sleep on Friday night too, but that didn't happen either." She leaned into her husband giving effect to what she had just said.

"Yea, you sure wasn't your normal self," clay responded with a smile.

"I don't hear you complaining either," Janice said with a little grin.

"Girl, after a night like that, I might not ever complain about nothing you do! I just hope it wasn't a onetime thing, because I could get used to this," Clay said.

"Well, then get used to it and a lot more changes, because things are gonna flip around here real soon," Janice said.

"Well, I'd better get started on this grass before it gets too hot to finish," Clay responded with a sigh.

But before he could get up, Janice pulled him close to her and said, "Don't worry about it, one of Daddy B's boys is on the way over here to cut it for us. We have somewhere to go! And before you say no, I can't go by myself. I need you to take me."

Clay looked into the eyes of Janice then said, "What are you up to woman?"

She couldn't hold it any longer. She'd kept quiet through all of their lovemaking and on through the night waiting for this moment. "I got a call yesterday from the hospital," she began, "guess who's gonna be a new daddy?"

Clay couldn't believe what he was hearing. After all these years, was it finally happening? "Janice are you for real?" was all he asked. Janice simply nodded as she grabbed him and both shed tears of joy together for the first time in a long while. They were on the road within an hour to go shopping at the larger stores in Marksville. What they couldn't find or decide on at the TG&Y or Gibson's department stores, they drove to Alexandria to the Sears and Roebuck store. Janice loved shopping here because she always got the feeling that the employees didn't have a major problem waiting on and helping black customers. By the time they drove out of the parking lot and back in route to home, both were satisfied with what they had purchased for the baby that would soon be theirs and it was quite a few items. The problem was that they were so excited they found themselves buying two of everything not knowing whether the baby would be a girl or a boy. Then they both settled on neutral colors like sky blues and soft greens and bright yellows. On their way home, they even joked about naming of the child.

"What about a crib, baby?" Janice asked. They already filled the backseat and some of the trunk with items.

"Call your sister and see what happened to that crib she had. It was smack brand new." Clay suggested. "Unless you think she plans on raising some more children?"

"I don't believe she plans on it", Janice answered. "I will call her when we get back home."

They rode in silence for the rest of the short trip home. When they pulled up in the driveway, they could see that one of Daddy B's sons had indeed cut all the yard. Clay pulled up as close as possible to the porch to make the unloading of the items they bought easier. He'd barely put the car in park when he heard Jean shouting at the top of her lungs for Janice. Janice hopped out of the car and shouted back over to Jean to come over and help her. Jean shouted back in the direction of her house for one of their children to tell Daddy B they had made it back.

"Girl, where y'all been this early in the morning?" Jean asked as she walked up and hugged Janice. "One-minute y'all was sitting on the porch, the next minute, I look up, y'all was gone. I didn't even see the car leave." Jean said all in one breath.

"We been shopping and I need you to help me put this stuff away," Janice told Jean.

Clay opened the trunk and began to take some of the bags out and get them on the porch while Jean and Janice unloaded the back seat.

"These two will wear anybody plumb out with their tongues," Daddy B said as he walked up to Clay.

The two friends shook hands and after Daddy B gave clay a hand taking the rest of the stuff out of the trunk, he shut it and they both went to go sit under the oak tree in the backyard.

"Ooh, Daddy, come and see, what all Janice have bought," Jean yelled through the living room window.

"Now, I'll leave that up to you. Besides, you'll talk my head off about it later," Daddy B replied.

At that, Clay laughed and Jean frowned at her husband that spoke volumes. Daddy and Jean had been married just a few years less than Clay and Janice, but their relationship had been a whole lot livelier in and through those years. They had a house full of beautiful children that were strong and healthy. Clay envied his old friend a little as he watched the continued closeness that he shared with his boys. He truly hoped that the baby that was on the way would be a boy. Just as he and Daddy B had sat down under the tree, there was a scream followed by laughter. Daddy B was about to get up to go see when Jean was hollering about, but Clay waved him down and pointed to the back-screen door signaling him to watch. After a minute or two, both women came out of the back door with a tray of iced tea and lemons.

"Daddy, guess who gone be a momma soon?" Jean blurted out as she reached her husband a glass of tea.

"It doesn't matter long as it ain't you again, "Daddy B said.

"Shut up fool. I ain't having no babies for you or nobody else for that matter." Jean said as she slapped Daddy B playfully upside his head.

"That's cause you all worn out and tired," said Daddy B.

"You were the one who wore it out, and it can't be that tired cause it knocked you clean out last night. The negro couldn't even get up this morning Janice." Jean snapped back.

I KNOW A BLESSING WHEN I SEE ONE

This was Daddy and Jean at their best. Playing the dozens at day until one or the other got tired or aggravated. Then that's when the real fights would begin, and those two could fight each other for hours. Then when they would finally simmer down, before they could apologize to each other, they'd be back in the bed going at it. Once Jean told Janice how she hated when she and Daddy would fight.

Janice had said, "Girl, I know you love that man too much to keep on hurting each other as y'all do."

"You right, Janice," Jean had replied, "but that's not why I hate fighting Daddy. As a matter of fact, I enjoy knocking him upside his head."

"Well, what's the problem then," Janice asked. Every time we get the best of each other in a good fight, then we get all hot and bothered, and before you know it, we back in the bedroom. Then there I go popping out another baby."

Clay laughed at the memory of the story when he looked at Daddy B and Jean. "Look, before you and Jean start World War II, we have something we want ya'll to know."

"Wait, Janice," Jean said, "he ain't never guess."

"Guess what woman?" asked Daddy B.

"You mean to tell me you done forgot what I asked you that quick?" Jean asked as she planted both hands on her hips as she started to get irritated.

"Look, I don't have a clue and as long as it ain't you, I'm happy," Daddy B said.

"Anyway," Jean began again, "Janice and Clay gonna be parents!" Jean was elated that she jumped into the arms of Clay and hugged him.

"Hey," Janice yelled, "you got yo' own man, you can't have mine too!"

"Janice, you know every time you mention babies around this woman, she goes slap crazy," said Daddy B. "But I'm very proud and happy for both of ya'll."

He got up to grasp the hand of his old friend Clay and he shook it with the vigor that was sort of an unofficial welcoming to the club that for a long time wouldn't accept Clay.

"Thanks, B, I feel great about it too," Clay said.

"Hell, you ought to, all this time you and Janice waited," said Daddy.

"Bernard Bridges, shame on you!" Janice exclaimed.

"Uh woman, hush. They know I mean nothin' bad. Clay, you and Janice been praying a long time and the Lord blessed y'all and even I can see that."

"Ain't no offense taken," Clay said. "Everybody here knows how Janice and I have been waiting and I know it's been a long time in the makin' but the Lord did seem fit to move now, and I'm just thankful," Clay concluded.

Janice looked at her husband in a new light. She'd never heard him speak so openly about how he felt about them not having kids, and to see him take the lead in giving an example of letting the past go, well to her it was utterly amazing.

"Amen to that," Janice said. "Look. Why don't we do a little celebrating while we still have a little time," Janice suggested to the others. "Lord knows once the baby gets here ain't no tellin' when we'll get another free Saturday afternoon like this."

"That sounds like a great idea to me, baby," Clay said as he jumped up and headed to the car. "C'mon B, let's go get some chicken and chops to throw on the grill, what'cha say?"

"I'm all for it. Jean get them boys to bring the grill over here and we'll get the fire started when we get back," Daddy B said while getting in the car beside Clay.

"Alright," Jean said as she walked towards the well-worn path that leads back to her house. "Janice, I'm gone get them potatoes and some eggs to make the tater salad. I'll be right back," Jean said as she trotted off to her house.

Janice went inside to start a pot of water boiling for the potatoes and eggs. Then she took out a five-pound bag of rice to wash and start it to cooking to make dirty rice. The screen door opened and shut as Jean came into the kitchen with a large bag of potatoes and a dozen eggs.

"You put the water on to boil yet?" Jean asked.

"Yeah. Sit down and let's get started on these potatoes. You make the dirty rice, and I'll make the tater salad," Janice said.

"You got a deal," Jean said, and from that point on, the kitchen was a whirlwind of activity.

Later on, that night, Janice laid in the arms of Clay thinking about what the baby would look like. She had always wanted a baby with a collection of features that reflected both of them equally, but at this point in their lives, it didn't matter as long as the child was healthy and sound. She mused over the desire to have a son rather than a daughter and how much easier it would be to raise a boy. But it still didn't really matter whether it would be a boy or girl. The main thing was that it would be their child forever. She smiled to herself and rested her head gently on Clay's chest. She closed her eyes and listened to her husband's breathing. Soon, very soon, their marriage would be complete. With this blessing from God on the way, she finally believed that nothing could take Clay from her again. With such thoughts, she drifted off to sleep.

CHAPTER 16

The alarm clock rang until Wanda reached over to silence it. She felt like taking it and throwing it against the wall, but that impulsive idea would get her nowhere fast. She lay there a few more minutes thinking about all she needed to do. She wasn't looking forward to going to work at 3 o'clock this afternoon, but she'd switched shifts with a co-worker in order to be off on Sunday. She eased up to a sitting position in her bed and looked around her bedroom. She swung her legs out of the bed and sat there for a few minutes. She picked up the pictures of her son that she kept on the nightstand by her bed. She looked at his picture admiring his handsome smile and those deep brown eyes. The folks back home all agreed that he had the eyes of an old soul. All Wanda knew was that they were beautiful.

"Good morning, momma's love," Wanda said to the picture as she kissed it. She really enjoyed a couple of weeks that he had some downtime to be with her, and now that he was gone, she yearned to be with him. "Someday, baby," Wanda said to the picture as a tear rolled down her cheek, "someday real soon!"

She got up and walked to the bathroom and looked at her disheveled hair and sighed. She'd get Sheila to press the hot comb through her hair sometime this morning. She turned on the water and let it run for a few minutes until it got warm. The running water urged her to use the toilet and when she finished the flush, it helped the warming of water. She went through the rigors of the early morning preparations. After she finished with her teeth and face, she went back to the bedroom to get dressed. She opened her dresser drawer and pulled out an old brown scarf and proceeded to wrap her head up until later. She then tied it in a knot at the back. Then she pulled on a pair of jeans she'd laid out the night before along with a nice button-up blouse. She sat down and slipped on a pair of tennis shoes.

"Good morning!" Sheila mumbled as she passed Wanda's room heading towards the bathroom.

"Good morning, cousin!" Wanda's reply began, "I don't think we look absolutely smashing this morning." Sheila just growled something in the direction of Wanda and kept going. Wanda finished tying her tennis shoes and then got up to go to the kitchen to start breakfast. She'd just taken the milk out of the refrigerator when the phone rang.

"Hello," Wanda said rather crossly. She couldn't understand why people had to talk so early in the morning, especially when the conversation wasn't that important, to begin with.

"Well, good morning to you, too!" Katie said to Wanda.

"Sorry, honey, but you know I'm not good in the mornings. What's up with you," Wanda asked.

"Oh, nothin' much. I woke up this morning feeling kinda anxious," Katie said.

"What do you mean anxious?" Wanda asked. She just finished pouring the milk over her bowl of corn flakes and was about to put a couple of heaping teaspoons of sugar in them.

"Oh, I don't know. It's kinda like when you got that feeling that something's about to happen," Katie explained.

"Kinda like when my left or right eye starts jumping," Wanda said.

"I never heard anything about a person's eye jumping," Katie laughed.

"You can laugh all you want, but it's still true. Every time something's about to happen to me, or for me or has anything to do with me, it happens." Wanda explained.

"So, you're telling me that every time something happens in your life, your eye jumps? Wanda, you gotta be pullin' my leg, right?"

Wanda continued to eat her cereal as she said to Katie, "You can laugh 'till you cry, it still doesn't change the fact that it's the truth. Furthermore, I ain't the only one who has this happen to them,"

Wanda continued as she got up to put her now empty bowl in the sink. "Black folks all around these parts can tell you stories about it."

Katie got a hold of herself as she realized that this was a serious issue that Wanda regarded. "Well, I heard enough stories about voodoo and witchcraft in these areas," Katie began, "I just didn't know that you believed in all that stuff."

"First of all, I didn't say anything about witchcraft and voodoo," Wanda started, "if you'd kindly be quiet long enough to hear me out then you might get a better idea of what I'm talking about." Wanda could feel herself becoming heated with Katie and it was apparent just how much by the increase of volume and change in tone in her voice. So much so that Sheila slid in the chair next to her. She gently placed her hand on top of Wanda's to calm her and inquire about what was causing her to get upset.

"I'm sorry for jumping the gun, okay, but put yourself in my shoes," Katie said to Wanda. "I didn't grow up around such things and I rarely heard of such practices until I came here," Katie continued, "and it hasn't been anything good that ever comes of it either."

"As I said, we don't practice anything. I and the rest of my family believe that God helps us," Wanda said.

"What do you mean, He helps you? He helps everybody, right?" Katie persisted

"That's right, but we believe that God can touch people to show them which way to go, or what to do even," Wanda continued.

She knew that Katie was completely lost and she definitely would prefer if her mother was here explaining this instead of her. Yet, she had to give it her best shot. Just as Wanda was trying to find the right words to say, her skin around and slightly above her right eye begin to twitch. So much so that even Sheila could see it.

"Katie, can you come over her right now? Please?" Wanda asked.

"Uh, sure. I guess," Katie said as she wondered what was going on.

"Try to get here as quickly as you can, okay?" Wanda persisted.

"Okay. Okay. I'm on my way, Bye," Katie said as she hung up.

"Wanda, what's up," Sheila said as she watched her cousin closely.

She was well aware of the shared belief within their family about God's toughing them. There was a time that she thought it was all a bunch of nonsense but over the past few years, well she'd begun to wonder. Her mother's left eye twitched for three hours last year and was about to drive her crazy until she got a phone call saying that her oldest brother's son had gotten killed when he fell into a sinkhole and was literally buried alive. Then there was the time that her right eye kept twitching until she went to the post office and there was a check for her in the mail from an organization sponsoring black people who were attempting to further their education. She hadn't even applied for the award, but still, in all, it was there.

"Wanda, what's going on," Sheila persisted. Wanda was starting to pace the floor. Something she never would do unless she was really upset about something. "Wanda, please say something," Sheila insisted. "You're making me nervous!" she exclaimed.

"I don't know what's happening or what's gonna happen," Wanda said as she absent-mindedly reached up to touch her jittering temple. As long as she could remember, it had never twitched like this. It was almost to the point of coming irritating.

"Sheila, call momma and see if everybody is alright at home," Wanda said. She forced herself to stop pacing and not to entertain some of the scary thoughts that kept popping in her head.

"Hello Auntie, how are you? It's me, Sheila. Is everything okay down there?" Sheila cupped the mouthpiece with her hand in order to relay what she heard back to Wanda. "She says everybody's fine on their end," Sheila told Wanda. "Ma'am, yes Ma'am, she's right here. Hold on." Sheila said as she reached the receiver to Wanda.

Wanda took the phone and took a deep breath before she said a word. "Hey momma, how you?" Wanda began. "Well, I just wanted to check on everybody and make sure all was well." She looked at Sheila with relief in her eyes as her mother told her that everybody was well, especially her son. "Yes, ma'am it's been jumpin' up a storm," Wanda said over the phone. "Sheila's fine and we'll be careful too. I'll call back tonight okay? I love you, bye," Wanda said and hung up.

Sheila was about to call her parents' house when a knock at the door caused them to jump. Wanda hurried to the door and realized that it was probably Katie at the door. Wanda hesitated for a moment as she wondered if it wasn't Katie. Her eye was still twitching even as she opened the door. Katie stepped in and looked at Wanda with concern.

"Wanda, what's wrong? Has something happened?" Katie asked while hugging Wanda. Wanda simply turned her head slightly and pointed to her left eye. Katie was about to ask what when she saw the muscles in the eyelash and around Wanda's socket twitch in a spasmatic way.

"Wow," Katie said. "Does that hurt?" she asked Wanda as she reached to touch it.

"No, it doesn't, but it's nerve-wrecking," Wanda explained.

Just then, Sheila came into the hall and said, "I just got off the phone with momma and everything's alright. I think we need to sit down and calm down," Sheila continued. All three went to the kitchen and Katie and Wanda sat down. Sheila went to the bathroom.

"Wanda, girl you had me scared half to death," Katie said. She watched as Wanda tried to make an effort to relax, but one could see that it wasn't easy. "Wanda, how long have these occurrences been happening in your life," asked Katie

"I don't know how far it goes back, but I've seen it all of my life," she told Katie as she leaned over and rested her head on the kitchen table. "Damnit, stop jumpin'!" Wanda shouted as she pounded the table with her fists.

"Calm down, sweetie," Katie said as she touched Wanda's arm. "We've all been under a lot of stress lately, so let's not add any through our imaginations," said Katie.

"You're right. I'm sure it'll past," answered Wanda.

"Wanda!" screamed Sheila as she burst through the bathroom door. "I know who it is this time," she said.

"Who?" both women said.

"Me! My water just broke!" cried Sheila.

CHAPTER 17

"Oh, my God!" shouted Katie as she jumped up from the table with such force that the chair fell backward.

"Oh, hell, I know something was gonna happen," Wanda cried as she reached over to help Sheila over to the couch.

"What's the date," Sheila asked.

"It's the thirtieth," Wanda answered after glancing at the wall calendar.

"We've got to get you over to the hospital as soon as possible," Katie said trying to keep her voice calm.

"Okay, but I'm not in any pain or anything so we don't have to rush," Sheila said.

"Okay then," Wanda began, "Katie go with Sheila to get her hospital bag, and I'll go and get us a ride!"

"Why don't we just call a cab," Katie suggested.

Sheila smiled at Katie and shook her head. "Girl, by the time a cab gets here I would've had the baby and nursing it too!" Sheila said.

"I can get my things. You call the hospital and tell them we're on the way," Sheila said over her shoulder.

"Are you sure you can manage?" Katie asked.

"Katie, I ain't gonna have the baby this very minute. Just make the call to the hospital and let Dr. Gray know that it's time." This was it. Sheila was finally gonna have her baby. Katie dialed the hospital and waited for an answer.

"Hello, this is Sister Katie Wells. I'll be coming in with Ms. Sheila Thomas who's scheduled for delivery and her water broke about five minutes ago," Katie said in a rush of words. "No, not at this time, but I will try to keep track once they start. Thank you. Oh, and she is one of Dr. Gray's patients, so please notify him of the situation. Yes, I'll see you soon. Goodbye," Katie said and hung up.

At that moment, Wanda came back into the house with her neighbor Raymond Brown in tow. "Where the gal at Wanda?" he asked as he searched the living room.

"Right here, Mr. Brown," Sheila said as she came through.

"Mercy me," Raymond said, "gal you look like you ready to pop!"

"Sheila how you feelin'," Wanda asked as she took the suitcase out of her hand.

"I really don't feel bad, it's just that I keep getting these muscle spasms right here," Sheila said as she pointed to her abdomen.

"How long has it been hurting like that," Katie asked as she pulled out a pen and pad to write the time down.

"What she doing with the pad," Sheila asked as they headed towards the door.

"She's keeping track of your contractions, stupid!" Wanda said.

"I'm not having any contractions yet; I just need to go poo!" Sheila responded. "Look, y'all getting too worked up. It ain't even began.... oooh!" Sheila couldn't finish her sentence as the pain shot up her body so quickly that she'd bent over and shouted all at the same time. "Damn, that shit hurts!" Sheila exclaimed as she tried to straighten up again.

"Gimme that case Wanda, and I'll be waitin' in the car," Raymond said as he took the suitcase and walked out.

"We right behind you, Ray," Wanda shouted after him. "Katie help her down the steps to the car. I have to make a quick call and lock up." Wanda said as she picked up the receiver.

"Wanda, you gonna call momma?" Sheila said as she crossed the threshold.

"Yeah, now quit!" Wanda said in that take-charge manner she always displayed. She hurriedly dialed Sheila's house and told her mother that Sheila was going into labor and that they were on their way to the hospital. Then she called her mom who picked up on the second ring. "Hello momma. I can't talk long, but my eye stopped jumping. I'm on my way to the hospital. Sheila's having the baby. I gotta go, bye."

Wanda hung the phone up rather abruptly but she was in a hurry. She grabbed her purse and house keys and headed to the door. She stopped briefly in the front of the hall mirror and quickly readjusted her scarf. She reached into her purse and put on some lipstick and puckered up as it ready to give someone a big fat kiss. "Never can tell," Wanda thought to herself, "might even find my Mr. Right." She smiled to herself admiring her face but, before she could do anything else, the sound of Mr. Brown's horn blowing jarred her back into the immediate situation. She grabbed everything again and ran out of the door. She pulled it behind her and locked the door.

"Look, you ain't got time to be putting on all that stuff on yo' face," Sheila exclaimed. She was clenching her teeth against the pain. "Catch a man on your own time, not mine," she shouted at Wanda. And with that, they were off to the hospital.

"Damnit to hell, hurry up!" Sheila screamed in the direction of Dr. Gray as he seemingly took his time checking her vital signs before she delivered.

"Now, just simmer down gal. It'll all be over before ya know it," Dr. Gray said. He looked at the clock on the wall. It was twenty minutes after four and Sheila's labor pains were coming at a rate of about every thirty seconds. "Okay young lady, I want you to put your feet in the stirrup and slide down a bit. There you go." Dr. Gray said as he positioned himself on the stool at the foot of the examining table. Sheila was sweating even though the air conditioner was on. She'd promised herself for the umpteenth time that if she could get through this, she'd never had another child ever.

"Uggh!" Sheila screamed as she clinched the rails on the side of the table.

"That's a good girl, now push again," Dr. Gray said.

"Wait doc, I gotta use the toilet now!" Sheila said.

"Go right ahead. It'll all come out in the wash."

"C'mon. Answer the phone already," Katie said as she let the phone ring a couple more times before she hung up. She'd been trying to reach the Jacobs at their home since arriving at the hospital.

Between running down to her office and back to the ward where Sheila was the time had slowly ticked away. She sat for a minute trying to catch her breath before getting up to head back to the ward. Katie closed her eyes for what she thought was only a fraction of a second when she heard her name called out.

"Sis Katie, oh I'm sorry. Were you praying?" Katie jumped but gathered her composure when she saw that it was only Sis Monica.

"You didn't interrupt me at all," Katie responded to her. "What can I do for you?" Katie asked.

"It's the Reverend Mother," the girl began, "she insists that you call her immediately when the Jacobs have arrived. I would have called, but I couldn't reach you over the phone so I came down to tell you."

"Thanks, Monica. I really appreciate it," Katie said.

"No thanks necessary, if I can help, I'd be glad to," Monica said then paused and said, "Well, if you need anything, just call."

She began to back out the door and was about to leave when Katie called her back. "Monica, wait," Katie began, "I really wanted to say thank you for covering for me and you. I know that Reverend Mother has been breathing down your neck to give her the names of who told Sheila about the Jacobs and the James families." Monica stepped back into the office and then, shut the door behind.

"Katie when you first arrived none of us welcomed you with open arms," Monica recalled. "We were downright mean to you and for my part, I'm truly sorry. We've been so caught up in keeping Reverend Mother happy that we forgot about pleasing God." Katie let that sink in, but before she could respond Monica began again.

"Don't worry. I'm keeping Mother so busy she can't remember what she did or said just yesterday. We're safe. I'll see you later Katie." And with that and a warm smile, Monica opened the door and left.

Katie stood there for a few more seconds thinking about all what Monica had said. It was true that she was treated like a complete outsider when she first came and up to this point many of her sisters till hadn't warmed up to her. But today, Katie was sure that she had at least one friend in the abbey. She smiled to herself, then went back to the phone and started to dial the Jacobs number again. She closed her eyes and whispered a quick prayer in hopes that someone would pick up the phone. On the fourth, someone picked up.

"Jacobs residence," was the words that Katie longed to hear.

"Hello, yes, this is Sis Katie Wells and I'm calling for Mrs. Janice Jacobs," Katie said.

"Hold on for one minute," the voice said. She could hear the woman who'd answered the phone calling Janice to come quickly to the telephone.

"Hello, this is Mrs. Jacobs," Janice said.

"Janice, this is Katie Wells. Can you and your husband come up here for tomorrow? The baby's mother is in labor even as we speak," Katie said.

"Oh, my Lord, yes! We'll be on our way either tonight or first thing in the morning," Janice said.

"Tomorrow morning will be just fine. I'll be waiting for you and Mr. Jacobs. See you then and congratulations," Katie said as she leaned back in her chair.

"Thank you, Sis Katie. We'll see you tomorrow. God bless!" Janice said and then hung up.

Katie eased the receiver down into its cradle and let out a sigh of relief. But before she could get out of the chair, the phone rang.

"Sis Wells speaking," Katie said.

"Please tell me you've heard from the Jacobs family," Monica said. She really sounded stressed out. Katie knew that the Reverend Mother was hounding her about it.

"Tell that woman the Jacobs will be here bright and early in the morning," Katie said.

"Thank God. I'll tell her now. Later Katie," Monica said and hung up.

As soon as Katie hung up, Wanda rushed into her office and blurted out, "She's pushing it out, let's go!"

"I'm right behind you," Katie said as she hopped up and followed Wanda out the door and on out the elevator.

"Congratulations, young lady," Dr. Gray said to Sheila, "you've done an excellent job."

Sheila felt like she'd lose consciousness at any moment. She was so exhausted. She couldn't believe it, but she'd done it. Her mouth felt extra dry and she tried to moisten her lips before she spoke.

"What, what is it doc?" She slowly asked.

"It's better that you don't know honey. Just know that this here baby is healthy and strong," Dr. Gray concluded.

Sheila tried to stretch her neck as far as she could to get a look at the baby. She only managed to catch a glimpse of the top of the baby's head. Whatever it was had black patches of curly hair. She thought about her hair and she simply smiled. She drifted off to sleep and dreamed that she was looking for something in the room that she and her sister shared growing up. She looked under the bed and then in the toy box where they kept the few toys that they had. Now she couldn't remember what she was looking for. That was strange. "Sheila, Sheila." Her mother was calling her but it didn't sound like her mother's voice.

"Sheila, Sheila. Honey, wake up!" Sheila opened her eyes and as her vision cleared, she recognized Wanda and Katie looking down at her. "Welcome back girl," Wanda said bending over to push the hair out of Sheila's eye.

"How do you feel, sweetie," Katie asked.

Sheila let that question process. She felt okay. Tired maybe, but still okay. She looked around the room and noticed a picture of water on the nightstand. She pointed to it and Wanda's understanding reached over and poured her cousin a glass of water while Katie helped her sit up in the bed. Sheila took small sips and lowered the glass.

She cleared her throat and said, "Thank God that's over!"

Katie and Wanda both laughed at Sheila's declaration. "Humph honey, the way you were moaning and groaning in there, I thought you and ole' Dr. Gray was getting' it on," Wanda said.

"Girl please," Sheila began, "after that experience, I don't want nobody pullin' nothin' out or puttin' anything in either!" Katie turned red, and Wand hooped at Sheila's comments. After the laughter died down, Sheila asked, "Katie have you and Wanda seen the baby yet?"

Wanda smiled as she sat on the bed next to her cousin. "Yes, and he's beautiful," was all Wanda said. She'd been briefed by Katie that it wouldn't be good for Sheila to know too much about the baby. It tended to develop into emotional scars later. "Sheila, I want you to understand that we're not trying to hurt you in any way, but it's best for you and the baby that the less you know about him the better off the both of you will be," exclaimed Katie.

"I guess it's too much for me to ask to see him. I mean just once." Sheila said with a pleading look on her face. She already knew what the answer would be, but knowing still didn't erase the fact or need to at least see the baby.

"Sheila," Katie began, "I'm not going to beat around the bush on this one. It's against policy for you to have any contact with the child after he's been born."

Sheila rolled her eyes and grudgingly said, "Look, it's not like I'm changing my mind or anything. I just would like to see him for myself," Sheila explained. She knew her chances of convincing Katie were slim to none, but maybe a little help from Wanda.

She looked over at her cousin who immediately crossed her arms over her chest and said, "No, don't even think it because it's not going to happen. We've got through all of this without any problems so don't you cause any!"

"All I'm asking is to see how he looks." Sheila persisted. She wasn't gonna give up that easily. Wanda bent over so she could look Sheila straight in the eye.

"The baby is fine with all ten fingers and ten toes. He's beautiful brown like you with brown eyes." Wanda said.

"With very soft brown soft hair and," Katie began but Sheila blurted out.

"Wait a minute. You've touched him?" Sheila asked with a strong edge to her voice.

"We both have," was the response from Wanda. "That's why we're telling you all this because we knew that you'd want to know."

Sheila just stared at the two women as if she didn't even know them. Before she could stop herself, she was sneering at both of them.

"Sheila, don't start," Wanda began. "You already knew the rules."

"But the rules don't apply to you?" Sheila shot back. She was in no reasoning mood and both Wanda and Katie could see that.

"Sheila, why don't you get some rest," Katie said. "I'm sure once you've rested a bit more then you'll see the logic in all this."

Sheila just sat there and looked from Katie to Wanda and back to Katie again. Sheila scooted back down into the bed and pulled the covers up to her chin.

"Girl, stop actin' like a baby. This is the way it is." Wanda said. "Now your momma told me to tell you that she's on her way to see you, so she'll probably get here tomorrow." Sheila turned on her side and closed her eyes. She was in no mood to talk to either one of them any longer. Wanda got up and mentioned to Katie to follow.

"We'll see you tomorrow, honey. Sleep tight." Wanda said as she and Katie left out the room.

After a couple of minutes, Sheila shifted back on her back and them to a sitting position. "Traders. That's what they are both, traders." Sheila said to the emptiness. Then she smiled to herself and said, "We'll just see what tomorrow will bring." And with that thought, she settled herself to go to sleep.

Wanda and Katie stood in front of the elevator waiting for it to come back up to the third floor. "You know, we'd get to the ground floor quicker if we took the stairs."

Katie suggested to Wanda as they watched the indication lights on the wall console. It appeared that the elevator was in constant service between the basement and the second floor.

"I think you're right. Let's go," Wanda agreed.

They walked to the entrance that led to the stairwell and grabbed the door and began the long walk down to the first floor. Apparently, they weren't the only ones who'd thought that taking the stairs was a good idea.

"Wow," Katie said. "I guess everybody's tired of just waiting when they could be moving."

"Well, it makes good sense to get where you're going while the getting good. I mean, it's not like we had elevators all our lives. Right?" Wanda said.

"You got a point there sista'," Katie agreed.

As they descended the stairs, they couldn't help but take notice of the unusual amount of people coming and going.

"You'd think this building has no elevators," Katie commented.

"I told you, girl," Wanda began, "most people don't trust 'em. They think that they'll fail at any time, and I can't say that I blame 'em."

"You think Sheila's gonna be alright?" Katie asked. She was still picturing the expression on Sheila's face when they left her room.

"Girl, don't worry yo' nerves about Sheila. She'll be fine." Wanda assured her. "She just so used to have her way with everything and everybody."

As they continued to walk down the stairs, Katie noticed Sister Monica waving at her from the second-floor level. "Katie, I was just looking for you. Hello Wanda. How are you?" Monica said as Katie and Wanda stepped on the level.

"Hey, Monica. You doing good?" Wanda asked.

"I'm blessed. You guys been up to see Sheila?" Monica asked.

"Yeah, and she's doing fine," Wanda responded before Katie could.

"As a matter of fact, she should be sound asleep by now," Katie added. "Now what can I do for you?"

"Well," Monica began, "I tried to reach you at your office first, but when you didn't answer I figured you were visiting Sheila. I wanted to let you know that the Jacobs' family has arrived."

"Did you get a chance to speak with them?" Katie asked.

"Yes, I did. They called and the switchboard connected them with me, my love," Monica said. "They said they'll be over in the morning around nine."

"Thanks so much, Monica, for letting me know. As always, I owe you one," Katie concluded.

Monica smiled started back down the steps as she descended. "I just want to be helpful when I can. Goodnight." Monica said as they watched her go through the exit door at the lower level.

"Y'know, she is really a sweet person," Wanda said.

"I wish there were more like her," Katie commented as the two walked down the last flight of stairs. "It would make this place a whole lot more wholesome."

"So, are you going back to your office and try to contact the Jacobs?" Wanda asked.

Katie gave Wanda a side glance as they walked through the exit door and into the first-floor hallway. "No. I hadn't planned on going back to the office. They did tell Monica that they'll be here till the morning so I guess I will see them then. Why do you ask?"

Wanda paused for a moment as she looked at Katie as if she'd spoken to her in a different language. "Katie, I can't be around when they show up or at the least be here early to keep Sheila still. She's supposed to walk and get some exercise tomorrow and it wouldn't be good having her and Janice bump into each other," Wanda concluded. "The fourth of July has passed and I'm not looking for any bigger fireworks."

Katie leaned against the wall wither arms folded, painting a mental picture of what could happen if such a meeting would take place and the ramifications that would most definitely follow. She even pictured the two women in a full bloom argument and all the while Reverend Mother would walk right in the middle of it all and demand an explanation. Then it would surely all come out and she'd be expelled from the abbey and the hospital. Reverend Mother would get her revenge on her in a glamorous fashion. The Jacobs would divorce after all this. The worst part is how much the child would lose if such a thing would happen. Katie thought about all of this in a matter of seconds.

She looked at Wanda and then said, "That is something we simply cannot let happen." Wanda simply nodded as they both agreed.

CHAPTER 18

"Janice, you almost ready?" Clay asked for what he felt was the umpteenth time.

They'd been up since seven o'clock that morning getting ready to go back to the hospital to hopefully, as he thought about it, sign whatever papers were necessary to get their baby and go home. He had to be back at work in two more days. He sighed as he thought about the probability that other than the trip back home, he'd missed out on those first hours that would take place in the baby's life. He'd just come back from outside the motel where he'd smoked a cigarette and now, he was ready to go to the family planning office and pick up the baby.

"Janice, bring yo' tail on here! Damn woman, you gonna be late for yo' own funeral," Clay said.

"Baby, I'm comin'," Janice said as she hurried out of the bathroom. She was wearing her favorite blue pantsuit with a white blouse and a pair of matching navy blue open-toe shoes. She didn't wear a lot of make-up just the basic lipstick, a little rouge and that's it. She believed that too much makeup was like putting on a mask. She wasn't trying to hide her face, but accent it. She checked her hair one more time in the mirror that hung on the wall. Her hair was done up in a tight bun. This was what she called her business affairs look. She grabbed her purse and whirled around to face Clay and announced, "Done. You ready?"

All Clay could do was smile and shake his head. "Yeah, I'm ready. Let's go," Clay said while opening the door for Janice to walk through.

"Clay is everything in the car? We didn't leave anything did we?" Janice asked.

"The only thing that's not in the car and almost got left is you," Clay said as he opened her side door for her.

"Oh, you're just so smart this morning," Janice responded pitifully. "I hope you remember to be that smart when the baby is home."

Clay started the car and put the car in reverse. "As long as we keep him away from your side of the family," he said, "he'll be fine."

Janice hit Clay on the arm as they backed out of the parking lot and headed towards the hospital. The traffic wasn't too heavy this morning which was strange at this time of the day. There were school buses out picking up the kids bringing them to school. A couple of children were about to climb on to their bus as Janice waved at them through the car window and they waved back and hurriedly entered the bus. Janice thought about the children at the Catholic school that she taught. Soon she'd be back teaching them, but not before her own baby was safe in the hands of competent people whom she trusted. She had even considered not going back to work until the baby was at least three years of age, but she hadn't discussed that with Clay.

"Well, here we are," Clay announced as they pulled into the hospital's parking lot. "C'mon woman," he began, "let's go get our baby."

Janice was smiling from ear to ear as they got out of the car. It was pretty warm already for seventy thirty in the morning.

"Whew, it's hot already," Clay exclaimed. "I hope this doesn't take all day."

They began the long walk to Katie's office in a hurried manner. Both wishing that whatever minor paperwork was needed to finalize the adoption would be done quickly and they would be on their way back home with their child.

"Do you think that we need anything else?" Janice asked. "Maybe we should have put the car seat in first."

Clay looked at his wife with an expression of compassion mixed with exasperation as they began to climb the ramp to enter the building. "Look, baby, we've got enough stuff to last for a couple of months at least. So, stop frettin' over nothin'," Clay said.

They walked the rest of the way until they reached Katie's office and as they walked in Clay said, "And as far as the car seat, well that's what your arms are for." They knocked and waited for someone to answer.

Sheila was up bright and early and prepared to execute her plan to the fullest. She already knew exactly where the nursery was and what time the curtains were opened to view the newborns. She also knew about what time Katie came to work, which would be around 7:30 or 8:00 am, give or take a couple of minutes. Wanda was the problem. Sheila didn't know exactly what time she'd come up to see her. Even though visiting hours weren't until the afternoon, usually Wanda came by Katie's office first and they would both come to see her together. Sheila wasn't sure rather or not Wanda had to work this morning or later on that night. She sat on the side of her hospital bed plucking up her courage to do what she felt needed to be done.

"I'm the one who gave him to both of them," she mused to herself. "I should at least be allowed to see him once before Clayton and Janice get here." Sheila slid into her house slippers, got up and after putting on her robe headed out the door.

Katie hurried towards her office with a cup of hot coffee in her left hand and the adoption papers in the right. She'd stayed later than she'd planned at Wanda's last night. They'd talked and clowned around until it was two o'clock in the morning, but after a quick conversation on the phone with one of the co-workers, that had changed. So, they talked and laughed and talked some more. Now Katie was late for her own scheduled meeting this morning with Clayton and Janice Jacobs. She turned the corner that leads to her office and almost ran smack dab into Clayton Jacobs' arms as he steadied her from stumbling.

"Oh my. I'm so sorry," Katie begins with a rush, "excuse me for being late this morning. I didn't mean to keep you waiting so long."

It was Janice who spoke. "Good morning Sis Katie," Janice said. "We were just about to go downstairs to get something to eat. Would you care to join us?" she asked.

"That sounds fine," Katie responded. "Why don't you two go ahead and I will join you in a few minutes at the Donut shop across the street. I have to grab a couple more papers for you two to read and sign. Is that okay?" Katie explained in a calm but hurried manner.

"Okay then," Janice replied. "We'll see you in a few minutes."

The Jacobs continued on their way and Janice hurried on to her office. She unlocked the door and rushed in leaving the door wide open. She sat the cup of coffee down on the desk and walked over to the file cabinet to get the other forms.

"Hey, sleepyhead," Wanda said from behind Katie.

Katie jumped in the slightest manner. She hated to be caught off guard by anyone, even if it were a close friend. She turned and gave Wanda a look that would have caused a charging bull to cringe away.

"Wanda for the umpteenth time, stop sneaking up on people," Katie said through clenched teeth.

"Sorry girl," Wanda began, "but I love to see you jump."

"If you keep this up," Katie replied, "one day you'll see me jump on you and beat some sense into you."

"Oh, aren't we jumpy today. What caused you to get up on the wrong side of the bed this morning," Wanda asked. She took one of the peppermint candies out of the bowl on Katie's desk and sat down.

"Actually, Wanda now it is not a good time for you to be here," Katie said as she finished putting the rest of the adoption contract together. She kept looking down the hallway as if she expected someone to walk in at any minute. Wanda noticed it too.

"Katie, what's got you buzzin' so much? You keep looking at that door like you expect all of hell to breakthrough at any minute," said Wanda.

"Not hell," Katie begin, "but it might turn into it if the Jacobs come back in and find you in my office."

"Oh shit! They're here already?" Wanda said as she leaped out of the chair with a look on her face as if she were about to take off and run.

"Now who's jumpy?" Katie asked.

Wanda turned towards Katie and said, "Ya' know if it were any other time sister dear, I'd give you a good cussin' out. Ya' know that right?" Wanda thought then she swiftly walked to the waiting room entrance door and peeked out. Katie couldn't help but laugh at the way Wanda looked peeping through the door.

"Oh, now it's funny huh?" Wanda hissed back over her shoulder at Katie. "Where are they anyway," she asked.

"I sent them across the street to get something to eat and I'm on my way to join," Katie explained as she walked up and then pass Wanda into the hall. She signaled for Wanda to follow then she told her, "This will probably be the last time you get to see the baby so you better hurry up to the nursery and say goodbye."

"Right, and I will swing by Sheila's room to check on her while I'm up there. I'll see you later then," Wanda said over her shoulder as she headed for the stairs.

Katie followed her with her eyes until she disappeared around the corner, then she picked up her pace to go find the Jacobs.

"That's got the be it," Sheila said as she slowly made her way toward the curtain covered glass windows at the intersection of the hall.

She hadn't been completely sure, but she had a distinct feeling that the nursery was somewhere on the same floor that her room was located. All she had to do was find it. As she made her way to the adjoining wall, she saw a sign that read: HOSPITAL NURSERY – NO viewing until 9:00 am! Sheila slumped against the opposite wall. She'd made it all the way in hopes of getting a glimpse of the child she'd given birth to. She knew that the Jacobs would be coming soon to pick the baby up, but she had to see him at least once. "Just to satisfy my soul," she kept telling herself. She was about to turn around when she saw a door off to the side of the windows about two yards down the hall from the side. After staring at the door for what seemed like forever, she finally made up her mind to go and knock. She was about to try the knob when the door suddenly opened and a short plump nurse came out and startled her.

"Oh, hello child," the nurse said. She had the friendliest smile Sheila had ever seen. "I see you're getting some exercise and that's a very good thing, my dear. Wouldn't want to be laid up no longer than necessary," she said.

"Dang, she talks even faster than Monica," Sheila thought to herself.

"Yes, ma'am. I decided to walk around and have a little …." Sheila began to say but was cut off in mid-sentence.

"Oh, you've come by a little early to spend some quiet time with your baby. How sweet, but it's still a bit early for me to open the curtains yet," she said in one breathe. She looked at Sheila and smiled that beautiful smile and said, "Is it one of the girls?"

"No. I had a baby boy a couple of days ago," Sheila explained.

"Oh, and what a handsome child he is," the nurse exclaimed. "He is the only boy in the nursery as a matter of fact and he's such a good baby. Hardly every cry," she said to Sheila.

"Is it possible that I could see him? I won't be long I promise," Sheila pleaded. She knew that she may never get another chance like this one.

"I can do better child, come with me," she said as she led Sheila into the nursery over to a rocking chair. "Now you sit right there and I'll be right back with your bundle of joy," she said as she walked to where a row of cradles was lined up near the back of the room.

Sheila watched with anticipation as the nurse gently bent over one of the cradles and lifted out a baby, her baby. She slowly began to walk towards her with the baby until she was right in front of her.

"Here little one," the nurse said as she placed the baby in Sheila's arms, "say hello to your momma."

All Sheila could do was stare at this beautiful brown creation that had been placed in her arms. Tears began to well up in her eyes as she drew him close to her face. She cradled him in her left arm she toyed with his tiny fingers with her right hand. His face was so full and plump, yet he felt light as a feather. She looked into his eyes and immediately she saw Clayton Jacobs' eyes. Her baby had an old man's eyes. He had his father's eyes.

"Hi baby," Sheila whispered. "Welcome to the world," she continued.

As if in answer, the baby made a fist around Sheila's pinky finger. He was precious. She gently leaned over and kissed him on his head.

"Sheila, let's go, honey," was the words that grabbed hold of her and dragged her back to this reality.

The strained voice belonged to Wanda whose expression was a combination of fear and regret. Sheila looked from her cousin Wanda and back into the face of this tiny new life. A life that was a part of her.

"Sheila, let's go honey. It's time." Wanda urged with a voice of urgency. She walked over to where Sheila was seated and gently began to lift the baby from her arms. Sheila started to resist but Wanda met her gaze and whispered, "We have to finish what we started."

After the slightest hesitation, Sheila released her baby to Wanda who quickly placed him in the arms of the nurse who had been standing there dumbfounded by the event that had just taken place. Before she could say a word, Wanda had spun around to help Sheila to her feet and out the door. She'd made it a quarter of the way up the hall when she slumped into the arms of Wanda. Her tears flowed like a river trying to wash away the ache in her heart.

As they exited the elevator, Katie along with Janice and Clayton Jacobs headed towards the hospital's nursery. Janice took her husband's hand in hers and gently squeezed in anticipation of seeing the baby for the first time, the baby that would soon be their own to enrich their lives just as much as they would enrich his.

"Sister Wells, when do you think we can take the baby home with us?" Janice asked.

"Oh, if everything checks out and the paperwork is all finalized, maybe as soon as this afternoon," Katie replied.

"That would be great," Clay responded. "We could be on our way back home before nightfall."

"Katie is the baby okay?" Janice began. "You said if everything checks out. Does that mean that there are some problems with him?"

Katie spun around to face Janice and said, "I'm sorry if I didn't make myself clear. The baby is fine and we're just being safe by monitoring him. I assure you that everything is fine."

They turned the corner and saw a sight that shook them to their core. Katie froze as she found herself facing Wanda as she consoled her cousin Sheila in an embrace. Wanda's glance went from Katie's frozen face to the rigid expression on Clay's face and finally at the face of Janice whose look of curiosity and concern caused Wanda to quickly direct her glance and gently lead a still very emotional Sheila pass them. Wanda did her best to conceal Sheila from the couple by shielding her with her own body. She knew from the look on Clay's face that he had recognized her, but that wasn't much main concern. She had to get Sheila to pass these people and back to her room as quickly as she could. Katie suddenly snapped out of her brief frozen state and promptly began to engage Janice in fresh conversation about the baby. She walked in stride with Janice placing herself between the two women.

As Wanda eased by Clay, keeping Sheila between her and the wall, she stole a quick glance up at Clay. She pleaded with her eyes in the hope that he somehow understood. Then in a moment, they were past them and, on their way back to Sheila's room. Katie continued to talk with Janice as they neared the nursery. Janice halfway listened to what Katie was saying, but her mind was locked on the scene that she'd just witnessed. The woman who was crying in the arms of the other woman seemed completely destroyed. Her heart went out to her. The other woman looked almost familiar as if she'd seen her some place before, but couldn't remember where.

"Well, here we are," Katie announced as they walked up to the viewing windows. Katie gently tapped on the window and motioned that the nurse brings the crib closer so they all could get a good look at the baby. While the nurse was getting the crib in position, Janice found herself asking Katie about the woman they had just passed.

"Katie," she began, "I couldn't help but notice the two women that we passed up in the hall a couple of minutes ago," she began.

"They seemed to be coming from this direction and one seemed so grieved. Do you have any idea what was wrong with them?"

Katie looked at Janice and could see the genuine concern in Janice's eyes for Sheila. For a moment, she wondered what would Janice say if she knew the truth. If she knew that the baby that was about to bring such joy into her life was the reason one of her best friends was crying from a bleeding heart.

"I realize it's none of my business," Janice said. "I was just concerned," she concluded.

"That's okay," Katie responded as she glimpsed back in the direction they'd gone. Katie thought for a minute then simply said, "She lost her child."

CHAPTER 19

Sheila woke up wringing wet. Her throat was dry and she felt as if she'd just finished a race. She looked around trying to remember where she was. Sheila raised from the bed, took a deep breath and slowly swung her legs out of the bed and sat her feet on the cold floor. The sting of its chilliness helped bring her back to the present moment. She knew where she was again, in a hospital awaiting release. She eased herself out of the bed and slid her feet into her house slippers that Wanda had bought for her. She sighed as she stood and began to walk over to the bathroom. She found the switch on the wall and the light stung her eyes momentarily. She sat on the toilet and when she was finished, she remained there a few minutes trying to remember the nightmare she'd just awaken from. It was so real or at least seemed to be. She got up and went over to the washbasin to wash her face and brush her teeth. She looked at herself in the mirror.

"I've got to do something with this rat's nest," she mumbled to herself.

She finished taking care of her needs and went back into the room. She decided against lying back down for fear of having the nightmare again. She sat in the chair next to the window and stared out at the early motions of the city. She tried to remember the happenings of the day before. She thought about her baby. How beautiful he was, how he felt light as a feather in her arms. Her beautiful little boy. The baby boy that she'd given away. The tears begin to flow afresh and she knew that she had to pull herself together before Wanda came and found her in this state of mind. She reached over to the little table where a small boy of tissues was and took a few to wipe her eyes and blow her nose. She didn't feel any worse for now, but she still had to get past this feeling. This horrible emptiness that she was now feeling that all stemmed from going into the nursery and holding her child.

"Why the hell I didn't listen!" she said to herself.

She leaned back into the chair and after a few moments, she began to relax. She closed her eyes for a moment or so she thought and slowly slipped away into a sleep that opened the doors of her subconscious mind. There her nightmare was waiting. She was sleeping when she first heard it. Just on the edge of consciousness, she could hear the wails of an infant. She awoke and found herself in her old room back at her parent's house in Mississippi. She got out of bed and she could clearly hear the voice of a baby crying in the near distance. She walked hurriedly through the house searching for the wailing child. Then she realized that sound was coming from the direction of the front door. She ran to the door and flung it open just in time to see some people dressed in white getting inside of a car with a baby that was frantically crying. The baby's blanket was stained with blood and as she took a step towards the car, a sharp pain arose from the pit of her stomach causing her to double over in pain. When she stumbled back to her feet, to her amazement, she had blood stains on her dress and at that same moment the baby cried out again as if calling her to come and rescue him. Immediately, she was running towards the car just as they shut the door and began to drive off. She tried to run faster but her legs felt like cement. She tried to cry out for the driver of the car to stop, but even her screams seemed muffled.

"Stop please stop!" She screamed. Then Sheila awoke to the shaking of Wanda.

"Sheila, wake up baby, it's alright!" Wanda urged. Sheila began to refocus her sight on her cousin Wanda who seemed so blurry. Then she realized that she was looking through tear-filled eyes.

"Sheila, it's okay sugar." Wanda soothed her. "I'm right here."

"Wanda, where is..." Sheila began, but her throat was so dry she couldn't speak clearly. She tried to begin again but her voice sounded terrible. Wanda got up and walked over to the nightstand and poured some water in the cup that sat by the pitcher of water. She reached the cup to Sheila whose hands were trembling. She helped her steady the cup so she could drink from the cup.

"Take it easy, cuz." Wanda said as she placed her hand in her cousin's back to comfort her. Sheila reached the cup back to Wanda and began to get out of the chair she'd fallen asleep in.

"Wanda, what time is it?" Sheila asked.

"It's almost nine o'clock and check out time for you is eleven a.m. sharp," Wanda explained.

Wanda looked at Sheila as she walked back to the bed where she'd placed the house dress she would wear back to the house. She silently prayed that they could get out of the hospital without any more incidents. She found herself drifting back to the events of the day before and how she had found Sheila in, of all places, the hospital's nursery sitting in a chair rocking her son. The son whom she'd already placed up for adoption. She knew that they were more than fortunate to have gotten out of there without further incident. Then to have passed by Katie and see the alarm on her face as she led the Jacobs to see the child that they would be raised as their own. That was too close to have to go through again. Today, she would make sure that Sheila would get up and discharge without any glitches.

"Sheila, why don't you lie down and try to relax. The doctor will be coming around soon to check you out."

"Wanda, I'm sorry about yesterday," Sheila began as she moved the clothes off the bed to place them on the chair.

"Girl, what in the world were you thinking?" Wanda asked in a voice that was louder than she'd wanted it to be.

Immediately Sheila went on the defense as Wanda's question caused her to wince. "I wanted to see him that's all!" Sheila said with increased volume in her own tone. "I know I wasn't supposed to do that but hell, you and Katie went and seen the baby and y'all held him and all that."

"Yes, we did," Wanda explained in a milder and softer tone this time. "But we weren't doing it hurt you. I wish we'd never said anything about it, or even have gone in there, to begin with." Wanda expressed.

Both women were silent for a moment, then Sheila said just above a whisper, "Isn't he beautiful Wanda?"

Wanda faced her younger cousin and saw the sparkle in her eyes and simply smiled and said, "Yes."

Sheila fell into the arms of Wanda. Wanda embraced Sheila trying to ease the despair she realized that she was going through. She herself had gone through hell when she was pregnant with her son. The ridicule and scorn that she encountered from neighbors and even the other family members. With all the pressure she faced during her own pregnancy, she was glad that her parents decided to help raise her son. It was a load off of her in so many ways. She could always call home and talk to him, or hop on the greyhound bus and go see him for a few days. And once things were better, she would send for him and they'd be together from now on. At least that was her plan, but now when she thought about Sheila's situation, wow, there would be no connections or no one to call to check on the baby. No way, to go see him. No conversations would take place. She would only have a son in memory because he would be gone. Wanda at the moment of the weight of such revelation hugged Sheila even tighter than she expected.

"Wanda, you okay?" Sheila asked as she separated from the hug. She looked at Wanda and instantly knew that her cousin was thinking about all that she herself would have to face.

"Hey, I'll live. Right?" Sheila said with a half-hearted smile. "They'll be other children along with a husband who can help raise them and be a full-time father too."

"Yeah, and God is gonna bless you in a way that will be beautiful. You'll see!" Wanda declared. "Now let's get you ready for when the doctor makes his rounds, then we can get him to sign you out and then we can get outta here!"

Sheila got back into bed and tried to relax as she listened to Wanda go on and on from one subject to the next. She knew she was trying to keep her mind off of the baby, but that was growing harder and harder by the minute.

"Have you talked to Katie today?" Sheila asked during one of Wanda's brief pauses for breath.

"No not this morning," she responded, "but she's going to be here in an hour or so to meet the Jacobs and finish up the paperwork for the adoption." Wanda filed on her fingernails with an emery board she'd kept in her purse. She didn't want to look at Sheila because she knew what the next question would be.

"I guess they'll be leaving with the baby tomorrow or the next day, right?" Sheila asked in a whispered tone.

Wanda raised her head and looked at Sheila. "Well actually as soon as they finish whatever the paperwork is that's left, they'll be leaving with the baby."

"So soon? I mean damn, I just had him the day before yesterday." She exclaimed. She was sitting straight up in her hospital bed now. "What's the rush? Doesn't he have to be checked out by the doctor too?"

"He's fine," Wanda said.

Sheila felt frantic. She knew in her heart that this was going to happen and she had accepted it as fate, but that was before she went to the nursery. Before she saw him and before she held him. Things were moving too fast. They were going to take her baby away today and on top of that, they were putting her out before she could see him again. All of a sudden, the nightmare that she had earlier was coming fully back to memory. Sheila was about to speak when the door to her room opened and Dr. Grey and Katie walked through the door.

"Well, good morning ladies," Dr. Grey said to both women. He walked around the bed and asked Sheila to lie down so he could examine her. "So how are you feeling, Sheila. I see you've been eating and your blood pressure is back to normal," Dr. Grey continued.

"I feel great and I'm ready to go," Sheila declared with a smile that was a little too bright.

"Well, I believe we'll be able to let you leave in another hour or so. How's that sound to you?" Dr. Grey asked.

"It sounds good to me, Doc," Sheila responded.

Wanda leaned against the wall as she watched the conversation that took place between her cousin and Dr. Grey. She listened to the words Sheila said but for some reason to her, they didn't seem sincere. Wanda knew Sheila quite well and after the conversation that took place between Sheila and herself earlier, this sudden change of attitude was very odd.

"Good morning, Wanda," Katie said as she eased over to where Wanda stood. She hadn't said anything yet concerning yesterday's encounter but the question would come once the doctor left.

"Well, everything seems in order." Dr. Grey said. "I'm going to the nurse's station and get your discharge documents in order. You take care of yourself. You hear?" With that, he patted Sheila on the shoulder and turned to face Wanda and Katie. "Sister Wells are you ready to finish up these rounds?

"I'll be right with you, doctor. I need to have a word with my friends for a quick minute or two. Why don't you go on ahead to the nurses' station and fill those discharge forms out first? I'll be with you before you're halfway finished," Katie said as she walked him to the door.

"That sounds fine. You gals take care now," he said.

With that, he left the room. As soon as Katie shut the door behind him, she spun around and glanced at both cousins as they faced her. Wanda had moved over to Sheila's side and took her hand in hers.

"Before you say anything, Katie, remember where we are," Wanda warned. "We don't need any more incidents."

"Well, how about somebody telling me about the incident, because I sure as hell am interested to know why you two were leaving the nursery."

"Well, before you blow your top sister," Sheila began, "I decided to take a walk and before I realized it, I was in the window of the nursery. I was trying to see the baby through the window but the curtains were all but completely closed." Sheila said.

Katie looked at Sheila and thought about what she'd just heard. She sounded sincere, but still, there was something about her tone. Before she could say anything though, Sheila began again.

"I was starting back when Wanda found me." Sheila looked at her cousin for effect and continued. "If she wouldn't have shown up when she did, I probably would have passed out right there at the door."

"Well, at least you're okay now. Right?" Katie asked with some leeriness. Fine. When can I leave?" Sheila asked.

"As soon as the paperwork is complete," Katie replied.

"Good. When do the Jacobs come to get their baby?" Sheila asked as she got up and began to get dressed.

She picked up the dress from the arm of the chair and walked back to the bed and began to take off her nightgown. Wanda looked at Katie as to say…just let it ride. Katie's shoulders slumped slightly in resignation and then she turned towards the door to leave.

"Well, I'm going to catch up with Dr. Grey, but to answer your question, they'll be coming to pick up their baby within the hour, so I better get crackin'," said Katie.

"You comin' by the house later girl?" Wanda asked as Katie opened the door.

"If you guys want me to still come by," Katie said.

For some apparent reason, all of a sudden, she felt strange around the two women that she'd spend so much time with. Before she could entertain this line of thought any further, Sheila responded.

"Girl, don't be silly. Why wouldn't we want you to come over?" Sheila looked up at Katie and gave her a look that she truly hoped would ease her friend's mind.

Katie paused for a moment, then returned that crooked smile she'd shown so many times before. "No reason, I guess. See you two later," Katie said as she closed the door behind her to leave.

"Whew! That was close," Sheila said as she continued to get ready to discharge from the hospital.

"Yeah, and I wasn't in the mood to try to referee between the two of you about yesterday," Wanda said as she sat on the edge of the bed.

Sheila slipped on her shoes and walked into the bathroom to try to do something with her hair.

"Wanda, I swear if it wasn't a sin, I'd cut all my hair off and start over again!" Sheila said from the bathroom.

Wanda laughed at the thought of her cousin bald. "It wouldn't be so bad," she began, "you'd look like some of these women we saw in that magazine from Africa, remember?"

"Now, I ain't ready to be in touch with my roots that bad. Just do something with my head, 'specially this kitchen." Sheila said as she tried to comb the hair that grew at the bottom of the back of her head.

"We'll do something to it once we get back to the house," Wanda answered as she watched Sheila come out of the bathroom.

"Sheila, it'll be a little while longer before we go. Why don't you sit down and get a little more rest okay!"

"Girl, I'm fine. I'm trying to hurry up. I'll just tie this scarf around my head and be done with it", Sheila said she hurried back in front of the mirror.

She tied her head up in a nice set that she'd seen in a magazine. The knot was to the side with the tails tucked into it. She turned to Wanda and asked, "How do I look?"

"You look fine. Sheila, where are you going?" Wanda asked as Sheila went to the nightstand and began to put her belongings into her overnight bag.

Sheila didn't answer Wanda's question but replied with a question of her own. "Wanda, who gonna come and pick us up?"

"I told you, Ray, to hand around the house so he can hear his phone ringing when I call," Wanda responded.

"Good. Well, that's about everything that I came with," Sheila said as she shut her bag.

She walked back into the bathroom to double-check and then gave the room another quick once over, then she turned her attention to Wanda who by now was back on her feet again ready to do something, except she didn't know what.

"Why don't you go downstairs and call Ray and tell him he needs to head on over here to get us," Sheila said as she reached her bag over to Wanda. "Take this with you. I'll be right behind you in a minute dear."

"Sheila, I wanna know where you are going?" Wanda asked.

Sheila turned and opened the door then said, "It would be better if you didn't know."

"Sheila, girl if you going back to the nursery, you gone spoil it for everybody!" Wanda exclaimed as she crossed the room in three quick steps and placed one hand on the door and the other on Sheila's shoulder. "Listen to me. I can only imagine how hard it is for you right now, but you gotta let it go!" Wanda explained. "You're young and you'll have more children. I know you will."

Sheila stepped back into the room as Wanda shut the door then said, "Look. I'm not about to mess it up or spoil the adoption either. I just want to see my baby one more time while he's still my baby." Wanda began to protest, but Sheila continued. "Listen. I'm not going down there to steal the boy or nothing like that. This is something I just gotta do for myself. If I'm gonna have any peace with this, I gotta do this my way. Now either let me go or come with me, cause one way or the other, I'm goin'."

CHAPTER 20

Katie waited in the lobby of the hospital or the Jacobs. She checked her watch for the umpteenth time and started pacing the lobby floor. She wanted to get this process over as soon as possible and put this child in the arms of Janice Jacobs. Putting this behind them all would be a challenge, but she believed that their friendship would weather the storm. Yet, her mind continued to linger on the expression on Sheila's face from earlier that morning. For some reason, she just couldn't get that feeling out of her stomach that Sheila was going to do something that they all would regret.

"I've got to stop thinking like this," she said to herself.

Katie went to sit back down on the chair where she'd been sitting moments ago. As she sat down, she closed her eyes in an attempt to relax her mind. She felt a gentle tap on her hand and she looked up to see the one person she definitely did not want to see.

"Good morning, Sister Katie. My, it seems that you didn't get enough rest last night. Maybe we should lighten your workload." It was the Reverend Mother. God her voice could sound so unsettling at times. Katie thought as she simply looked up at her. She realized that had this have happened several months ago, she would have bolted upright in her chair and probably have broken out in a cold sweat, but that was then and right now she was too preoccupied to be intimidated by her superiority.

"Good morning, Mother. What brings you down here so early," Katie asked even though she believed that she knew the truth already.

The Reverend Mother turned and began to talk as she walked away from Katie, but to her unsettling surprise, Katie hadn't even made and attempt to rise or follow.

She spun and said, "Sister Katie, aren't you coming?"

"No, Mother. I'm waiting for the Jacobs to arrive." Katie replied.

"Ah, yes, the adoption is to be finalized today. Correct?" She said with an air of mock interest. "I assume that since you were so settled on this Jacobs family from the start that all of the documentation is in order?" She asked.

"Oh yes, Mother. Everything has been properly affixed regarding all points of interest." Katie's response was a bit edgy, just enough that Reverend Mother was able to take notice.

"Yes, I do hope so for all our sakes," was all the Reverend Mother said.

Before Katie could muster up a response, her attention was turned towards the stately couple that was even now approaching her. As the distance closed between, she and the Jacobs, she could see the joy radiating all over the face of Janice Jacobs. "And why shouldn't it," she thought to herself. She who had waited for so long was finally about to become what she longed for, a mother. Janice, Jacob's dream was finally coming true. She'd have her very own baby to love and raise for her very own. This was truly her blessing.

"Well, I can see that you both are ready to receive your very own bundle of joy," Katie said as Janice and Clay reached her.

"Good morning, Sister Katie," Clay began. "Is everything ready?"

"Yes, it is Mr. Jacobs. So, if you would just follow me up to the nursery, we'll go and get your son."

Just as they were about to leave, Reverend Mother stepped quite swiftly in the path of the Jacobs and between Katie and proceeded to introduce herself.

"Good morning," she said in a rather stiff tone. "I don't believe we've had the pleasure of meeting." She didn't extend her hand to shake Clay's hand that was already waiting.

Clay retracted his hand and at that moment Katie chimed in to keep an awkward moment from growing worse. She did a quick introduction of the Reverend Mother to the Jacobs and then proceeded to usher the family to the nursery. The Reverend Mother looked on as they disappeared around the corner. She turned and began to walk away, and then she slowed in her pace, turned and followed after Katie and the Jacobs.

Wanda walked nervously by the side of what now seemed to be a very confident and determined Sheila. She watched Sheila as she seemingly marched to the nursery and thought back to all the events that brought them to this point. Not to mention the people who'd come into their lives. People like Katie. A woman who likes them had been oppressed because of who she was. Katie who befriended Sheila on the bus that faithful morning. Katie who had shown herself to be a woman of integrity and faith. She'd done all that the possibly could to help Sheila and had become a true solid friend to both. Now Sheila was positioning herself for a head-on collision that could not only break hearts but turn worlds upside down.

"Sheila, what in God's name done got in that head of yo's?" Wanda asked in a hurried tone.

"I'm gone get what's mine," Sheila answered.

Wanda grabbed Sheila by the arm and held tight. "What you gonna get is some time to cool off in the city jail if you don't stop actin' crazy!"

"Look!" Sheila said, "He's still my baby and as I told you earlier, I gotta do this my way or else."

"Or else what, Sheila?" Wanda asked. "If you don't have yo' way, everybody else gotta suffa? You call that right? What about the baby?"

"What do you mean?" Sheila asked as she stood toe to toe with her cousin.

"Now listen, Sheila. If you wanted to keep the baby, well then, I'd be with you every step, but you decided to do what's best for the child and give him a chance to grow up better than we did. He'll have a nice home and good down to earth people who will love him and raise him right. He'll go to church and learn to read and write and finish school. He might even to college, Sheila," Wanda said. "Everything you said you wanted to give him; he can have with the Jacobs." Wanda took Sheila's hands into her own and firmly held them. "Sheila, let's go and let this child go where it will be best for him."

Slowly Sheila began to yield to Wanda's persuasion and after what seemed like a very long time, she allowed Wanda to lead her away from the place they stood. Wanda hadn't realized how close they were to the nursery and as she began to turn Sheila back in the direction they had come, the curtains of the nursery were opened. Wanda paused and looked over her shoulder at the now opened viewing area where the newborns would be. She almost was tempted to go and take a last glance at Sheila's baby. Sheila felt the hesitation in Wanda's movement and she slowly began to turn back towards the nursery.

"C'mon cuz, let's go. There's nothing here for us anymore!" Even as Wanda said those words the regret flooded over her.

"Nothing here?" Sheila said as she froze in the spot where she stood.

Wanda gently tried to tug at Sheila to start back down the hall without looking into the eyes of her cousin wishing she hadn't said the words that resonated with someone who was completely unfeeling towards the child she had given birth to.

"Nothing here," Sheila repeated in a much louder voice as she yanked free of Wanda's grasp.

"Sheila, I'm sorry that didn't come out right." Wanda tried to explain, but it was too late. Sheila was over the edge and already heading straight to the nursery.

"Sheila, stop! Girl, you gonna get us all in a heap of trouble!" Sheila stopped at the window and began to look from crib to crib for her baby.

"Wanda, I think you need to go home. I'll catch up with you later." Sheila said over her shoulder to Wanda. "I wouldn't want you to get in trouble foolin' around with me," Sheila said in a very cold tone.

"Sheila, you ain't thinkin' straight," Wanda said.

"My thinkin' is just fine, as a matter of fact, everything is clear."

"Sheila, now you listen to me. Katie gone be here any minute, with Clay and his wife. We can't stay here!"

"Look, I will only be a few minutes, okay. I wanna see my baby one last time." Sheila said to Wanda without turning away from the viewing window.

Sheila quickly scanned the room hoping that the nurse that was working the nursery the last time she was down there had the day off. The lady she saw was new and when she noticed her, she cheerfully waved at her as she went about her morning routine. Wanda was about to begin pleading with her when they heard voices coming from around the corner. It sounded like Katie, but they weren't positive.

"Sheila, let's go, girl! We can't take this chance."

"No! Not until I see him. Do me one favor," Sheila said in a rush of words. "Try and stall Katie if you can for a couple of more minutes."

"Are you crazy, Sheila?" Wanda asked.

Sheila began pushing Wanda towards the adjoining corridor where the voices were coming from. "Just go!" Sheila said in a voice of desperation.

Wanda knew Sheila was set on seeing that baby no matter what, even if it meant being caught by the Jacobs and Katie, which would be terrible. Right then, Wanda knew she had to figure out a way to stop Katie from dead in her tracks. As she hurried around the corner, she knew exactly what it would take to do so.

Sheila made it back to the window in time to see the nurse cradling a baby in a little blue blanket. Her heart stopped as she saw the chocolate-colored skin and something inside told her that this baby was hers. She needed a better look though and before she could think it through, she was at the nursery door gently knocking as she tried to turn the handle. Beyond all hope, the door was unlocked. Sheila walked in and found herself facing the nurse and the baby she held. Her baby. The baby she came to say goodbye to.

"Ma'am," the nurse began, "no one is allowed in the nursery without permission."

"I'm sorry," Sheila began as she shut the door behind her. "I'm discharging today, and I came to see my baby."

"Oh, well, why didn't you say so," she replied to Sheila. "I've, or should I say we, been expecting you this morning. I was told that Sister Katie was bringing you down," she continued as she looked over Sheila's expecting to see Katie.

"Uh, Miss Wells will be a few minutes. She had to go back to her office for just a moment, so I just came ahead of her."

"Well, good," the nurse said as she switched arms to hold the baby and shake Sheila's hand.

"How's the baby," Sheila asked.

"Oh, he's just fine. Strong and healthy. I was just about to feed him his last bottle before he leaves."

"I can hold him while you get his bottle." Sheila offered as she hovered over the baby.

"That would be such a help," the nurse replied. "I'll be right back. Here you can sit with him in the rocker."

Sheila reached out and took the baby and instantly began to rock with him. She eased into the rocker and began a slow gently rock that brought comfort to her as well as the baby. She moved the blanket from around his face to get a better look at him. She gazed upon his tiny face, marveling at his dark brown eyes, button nose, and a cute little mouth. Sheila gently kissed her son on his nose then his forehead and she drew him as close to her as possible.

"Is everything alright?" the nurse asked from the other side of the room.

"Fine, everything is just fine," was all Sheila could say.

Wanda rounded the corner at such a brisk walk, one would think if they saw her that she was about to break out into an all-out sprint. Wanda saw to her dismay the Jacobs and Katie approaching with of all people the Reverend Mother in tow. Wanda didn't know what she would do or say to them, but she knew she had to do something quickly or all hell would break loose. Wanda squared her shoulders and headed directly toward Katie, hoping that somehow, she could communicate to her what was going on without saying too much.

"Good morning Sis Katie. Where might you be going?" Wanda said in such a way that caused Katie, who had been chatting with Janice Jacobs to take notice. Wanda stopped directly in front of Katie looking only in her face, hoping that Katie could tell by her eyes that something was wrong.

"Good morning," Katie responded. She tried to look around Wanda expecting Sheila to show herself. "How are things going this morning for you and your cousin," Katie asked. You could hear the tenseness building up in her voice.

"Oh, she's not herself," Wanda said hoping that her own nervousness wouldn't raise attention from the others. Too late.

"Excuse me, young lady," Reverend Mother said as she stepped up to Katie's side. "Whatever the problem is, I'm sure it can be handled at another time. We are on a tight schedule and we can't keep these good people waiting."

And with that, Mother Reverend proceeded to place her hand in Katie's back and began to gently, but firmly push Katie forward until Wanda had to move out of the way. The Jacobs followed close behind and passed by Wanda but now without Clay taking a quick glance at Wanda. There was an urgency in his eyes. An urgency that Wanda had been feeling for the past few minutes. The kind of urgency that spoke of oncoming dread. All Wanda could do not was hope beyond hope that Sheila had left the nursery, but what they would all find would change the whole situation.

Even as Wanda fell in step with the others, Sheila sat in the nursery holding and rocking her baby. She knew that she had to leave before all hell, break loose, but she just couldn't stop gazing in her son's eyes. He began to gently cry. The sound of his cry and the little tears that formed at his eyes threw Sheila into a panic. What could be wrong with him, she wondered. She was about to call the nurse when the strangest thing happened. At the angle Sheila held the baby, his tiny hand had brushed against her exposed skin across her chest. At that very moment, she knew what was wrong with her baby. He was hungry and needed to be fed. She needed to feed him. She could feed him right now. It would be so easy. There was no time and she knew Wanda would not be able to stall Katie and the Jacobs any longer. Sheila closed her eyes to fight back tears that she knew were inevitable. She began to unbutton her blouse until she reached the lower portion of her bra. Then with her left hand, she reached into her bra and pulled out her right breast and placed her nipple into the baby's mouth. He began to such immediately.

Katie and the Reverend Mother turned the corner together and faced the viewing window together with the Jacobs. The nurse could be seen bustling around the babies that were already placed in the viewing area. She looked in their direction and smiled as she opened the nursery door for them to enter.

"Well, good morning Reverend Mother," the nurse began. "I wasn't expecting to see you with Sister Katie. I know you've come to pick up the baby and I have him all ready to leave."

Katie blinked back the question that kept echoing inside her head. "Where was Sheila?" Before she was able to continue down that train of thought, she heard the Reverend Mother demand where the baby was and why wasn't he in the viewing area.

"Well, I would have had him up here, but his mother came by and…." the nurse said but was cut off by the Reverend Mother.

"What are you babbling about, the child's mother!?"

"Well, I'm sorry", the nurse began, "but I didn't think it was a problem with her coming to get the baby and all."

Katie placed a firm hand on the nurse's arm. "Sister, where is the baby now?" Katie asked with a voice filled with tension.

"That's what I'm trying to tell you, Sister Katie. She's right here holding the baby." The nurse began to lead the two to where the baby was.

Before she could, two very unexpected things happened. First Sheila came from around the corner with the baby, her baby which she was about to give to the man whom she'd conceived this beautiful baby boy with and the woman he was married to. The woman who would raise her child. The woman whom her son would look to and call the mother. The thought alone was enough to cause her to clutch the child which was concealed by the diaper that covered his head.

"You little witch!" the Reverend Mother hissed at Sheila. "How dare you. Give me this child...."

But before she could finish her sentence, the second thing happened. The door to the nursery swung open abruptly and Janice and Clay came in to see a sight that caused Janice to faint, Katie to gasp, and Wanda to moan in dismay.

"I will give him to Katie as soon as he's finished eating," declared Sheila. With an estranged look in her eyes, she gently uncovered the baby's head to reveal him suckling at her breast.

"Sheila, how could you!?" was all Katie could muster to say.

"You, treacherous girl!" the Reverend Mother began. "May God have mercy on you."

Sheila looked up from the baby with a smile on her face and simply said, "He already has."

This ends book one of "I KNOW A BLESSING WHEN I SEE IT" series. Be on the lookout for book two: 'CURSED BUT STILL BLESSED" coming soon.

www.ingramcontent.com/pod-product-compliance
Lightning Source LLC
Chambersburg PA
CBHW030118100526
44591CB00009B/438